Globalism and Gendering Cancer

This book connects a rhetorical examination of medical and public health policy documents with a humanistic investigation of cultural texts to uncover the link between gendered representations of health and cancer.

The author argues that in Western biomedical contexts, cancer is considered a women's disease, and their bodies are treated as inherently oncogenic, or cancer producing, which leads to biomedical practices that adversely impact their bodily autonomy. She examines how these biases traverse national boundaries by examining the transmission of biomedical cancer practices from the US and international organizations to Kenya.

This book is suited to scholars and students working in the fields of rhetorics of health and medicine, medical humanities, and gender studies. It is also of interest to medical professionals and readers interested in globalism and global health.

Miriam O'Kane Mara is Associate Professor of English at Arizona State University. Her research interests include medical and health discourses, Irish literature and film, and food studies. In all of these contexts, her work examines the intersections between landscapes, bodies, texts, and discourses. She has been published in *Technical Communication Quarterly*, *New Hibernia Review*, *Feminist Formations*, and *Irish Studies Review*.

Routledge Focus on Communication Studies

A Relational Model of Public Discourse
The African Philosophy of Ubuntu
Leyla Tavernaro-Haidarian

Communicating Science and Technology through Online Video
Researching a New Media Phenomenon
Edited by Bienvenido León and Michael Bourk

Strategic Communication and Deformative Transparency
Persuasion in Politics, Propaganda, and Public Health
Isaac Nahon-Serfaty

Globalism and Gendering Cancer
Tracking the Trope of Oncogenic Women from the US to Kenya
Miriam O'Kane Mara

Globalism and Gendering Cancer
Tracking the Trope of Oncogenic Women from the US to Kenya

Miriam O'Kane Mara

First published 2020
by Routledge
52 Vanderbilt Avenue, New York, NY 10017

and by Routledge
2 Park Square, Milton Park, Abingdon, Oxon OX14 4RN

Routledge is an imprint of the Taylor & Francis Group, an informa business

© 2020 Taylor & Francis

The right of Miriam O'Kane Mara to be identified as author of this work has been asserted by her in accordance with sections 77 and 78 of the Copyright, Designs and Patents Act 1988.

All rights reserved. No part of this book may be reprinted or reproduced or utilised in any form or by any electronic, mechanical, or other means, now known or hereafter invented, including photocopying and recording, or in any information storage or retrieval system, without permission in writing from the publishers.

Trademark notice: Product or corporate names may be trademarks or registered trademarks, and are used only for identification and explanation without intent to infringe.

Library of Congress Cataloging-in-Publication Data
A catalog record for this book has been requested

ISBN: 978-0-367-19810-7 (HB)
ISBN: 978-0-429-24338-7 (EB)

Typeset in Times New Roman
by Apex CoVantage, LLC

For Andrew

Credit: Miriam O'Kane Mara

Contents

List of Figures viii
List of Tables ix
Acknowledgments x

1 Introduction: Rhetorical Checkpoints 1

2 Oncogenic Women in a Cancer Culturescape 21

3 Tracing Kenya's Culturescape: Cancer as Gendered Weakness in *Place of Destiny* 45

4 Kenyan Healthscapes: Oncogenic Women in the Nairobi Cancer Registry 62

5 Kenya's Health Professionals Speak: Attitudes About Cancer in the Field 88

6 Conclusion: Saratani Going Forward 108

Appendices 113
Index 121

Figures

2.1	Breast cancer semipostal stamp	26
4.1	Nakumatt "Let's Fight This Battle Together" poster inside Nakumatt supermarket	64
5.1	Hospital triage and phlebotomy room from research site	89
5.2	Who gets cancer the most: frequency bar chart	91
5.3	Who suffers the most from cancer in Kenya: frequency bar chart	91
5.4	Who is most likely to die from cancer in Kenya: frequency bar chart	92

Table

2.1 News media coverage of mammography overdiagnosis findings 31

Acknowledgments

Parts of Chapter 2 were first published as "Spreading the (Dis)ease: Gardasil and the Gendering of HPV" in the *Feminist Formations*, 22.2 (2010), 124–143. Reprinted with permission by Johns Hopkins University Press.

Parts of Chapter 5 were first published as Mara, Miriam, and Mara, Andrew. "Blending Humanistic and Rhetorical Analysis to Locate Gendered Dimensions of Kenyan Medical Practitioner Attitudes About Cancer." *Technical Communication Quarterly*, (2017), 1–15. Reprinted by permission of the Association of Teachers of Technical Writing, www.attw.org.

I would like to acknowledge and thank Christi McGeorge at North Dakota State University for her generous help with the interview instrument and SPSS analysis.

I would like to acknowledge and thank the Fulbright Scholar Program and the Council for the International Exchange of Scholars (CIES) for their support, without which this project would not have been possible. The interviews were conducted during a Fulbright.

Special thanks to the researchers and health care professionals at KEMRI and elsewhere, my colleagues at Kenyatta University, and the people of Kenya who allowed me to share their space and answered my questions.

1   Introduction
Rhetorical Checkpoints

Introduction

In 1995, Laura Pemberton was compulsorily removed from her home and forced to undergo a cesarean section after previously fleeing a hospital where they planned to sedate her and conduct a cesarean section. After leaving the hospital, she had been proceeding with a vaginal birth at home, when a consulting doctor at Tallahassee Memorial Regional Center, with the hospital itself, sued. They had decided that only a cesarean birth would be safe for the fetus because of Pemberton's previous C-section. The medical professionals argued that the fetus's rights outweighed Pemberton's rights to choose or deny health care services. The sheriff's department dispatched officers to her home, who subsequently physically disabled her from laboring and took her back to the hospital. Once there, she was allowed to represent herself, while the court appointed a lawyer for her fetus, in a hearing that resulted in overriding Pemberton's right to bodily autonomy and mandating a surgical procedure against the patient's expressed wishes. Pemberton subsequently sued and lost. In Pemberton vs Tallahassee Memorial Regional Center, Judge Hinkle asserts that the state has an interest in protecting the fetus.[1]

Autonomy's Limits

Such cases are extreme, but they demonstrate how women's individual well-being can be constructed as if they are in opposition to positive public health outcomes in biomedical contexts. Feminist researchers in medical rhetoric like J. Blake Scott reinforce such constructions in the context of routine HIV testing of pregnant women, arguing that testing "render[s] some pregnant women and new mothers as threats to rather than members of the national citizenry" and enables "the subjection of these women to various forms of oppression, from compulsory testing and treatment to criminalization" (Scott 161). Michel Foucault, who assembles medicine as a disciplinary practice, explains that "in the process of hysterization of women, 'sex' . . . constitutes woman's body, ordering it wholly in terms of the functions of reproduction and keeping it in constant agitation through the effects of that very function" (153). Thus even non-pregnant women's private medical decisions can collide with other interests within the complexity of biomedical contexts, where networks of information, people, and technologies create categories of risk. Adele Clarke and her co-editors define biomedicalization in contrast to medicalization, suggesting that it goes beyond medicalization's "emphasi[s] exercising control over medical phenomena – diseases, illnesses, injuries, bodily malfunctions" toward "transformations of such medical phenomena and of bodies" (Clarke et al. 2). Importantly, they describe one focus of biomedicalization as "the elaboration of risk and surveillance at individual, niche group, and population levels" (Clarke et al. 2). In this tradition of medicalization and biomedicalization, women and women's bodies can be held responsible for monitoring and submitting to medical interventions to protect and transform their own health as well as the health of the community.

Building out from biomedicine "as a shorthand expression for the interactive field of science, medicine and health care" (Shildrik 6–7), public health as a field focuses on social interventions to solve health-related problems, such as smoking-cessation campaigns to combat lung cancer. Unlike clinical medicine's focus on one patient at a time, public health professionals concern themselves with the health of a community as a whole, sometimes at the behest of government organizations through policy. Public health professionals would usually be more receptive to environmental explanations and interventions rather than a strict biomedical emphasis on genetic or personal risk. Yet, the biomedical model inflects public health structures. As Mamo et al. explain in "Producing and Protecting Risky Girlhoods" "this imperative [to accept biomedical interventions] is especially evident as the role of public health is increasingly privatized" (124). Sometimes, in public health, women are targets of education and other efforts because they are seen as responsible for their own health and the health of families. Mamo et al. name this phenomenon "a feminized collectivity responsible for protecting the nation's health through body practices" (134). In other words, women's bodies may be subjected to medical interventions if such interventions are deemed necessary for the public good, and thus, women's bodily autonomy has potential to be undercut by both public health policy and biomedical requirements for bodily improvement and management of risk.

Public health practitioners articulate health concerns in terms of populations, depending upon epidemiology and statistics, but this emphasis on populations sometimes means that certain groups are targeted for policy intervention to benefit other groups. Many incidences of such interventions sacrifice women's bodily autonomy for existing or potential fetuses. Autonomy or self-rule represents the ability of patients to access and obtain – or deny – screenings, treatments, or other health care products and processes, deciding for themselves what health choices are appropriate. It is one of four bioethics ideals that include beneficence, non-maleficence, and justice in addition to autonomy. These concepts allow bioethicists to evaluate medical practices and technologies for moral implications, and they can provide a conceptual frame for feminist rhetorical investigation of documents that implement biomedical movement. Clarke et al. suggests that "the rise of bioethics and patients' rights movements of the 1970s sustained these critiques [of biomedicine]" (15). Bioethicist Karla Holloway maintains that autonomy as "the first in the four principles that guide traditional bioethics" connects deeply with identity, which becomes clear when "gender and race are at issue" (17). While a biomedical intervention may already sidestep the issue of individual autonomy because of its focus upon larger collections of people, the issue of autonomy especially gets nuanced for women in conjunction with pregnancy and childbirth. While this may seem an esoteric distinction, the Pemberton case illustrates the very real ways that biomedical assumptions already inform medical, juridical, and police interventions; women in the United States can be arrested and lose other rights if they do not attend to medical care while pregnant. In some cases, pregnant women are incarcerated for drinking alcohol or using other recreational drugs.[2] In other cases, doctors have mandated bed rest for pregnant women, even those who cannot afford to take time away from work.

Biomedical justification of autonomy-restricting medical and juridical interventions are neither new nor isolated. The mandated cesareans of women like Pemberton may be read alongside the public health edict to vaccinate only women and girls against Rubella, a measles virus that can cause congenital defects; both types of interventions attempt to protect fetuses through medical procedures on women.[3] In some cases, not just fetuses or vague public health claims, but the status and agency of the medical field itself gets considered more important than the autonomy of the woman. As Foucault reminds us, "the medical examination" and other "controls . . . function as mechanisms with a double impetus: pleasure and power. The pleasure that comes of exercising a power that questions, monitors, watches, spies, searches out, palpates, brings to light" (45). This power circulates through women's medical interactions with health care. In some interactions, evidence does not favor secondary cesarean section and women may wish to attempt natural labor, but many physicians recommend secondary cesarean as a matter of course. Thus, women's decisions are overridden not just for the sake of the fetus but for the sake of the autonomy exercised by the medical field, which ironically builds its ethos on claims that are supposedly evidence based. Yet beyond protection of fetuses, women's bodies bear the responsibility for public health in other contexts; even in non-reproduction instances, medical interventions are often prescribed for women more easily than for men. Of course, using a binary of women and men can erase the experiences of non-binary and trans people in their experience of biomedical environments. Elizabeth Grosz explains that "a plural, multiple field of possible body 'types' . . . must be created" (22), while primarily maintaining a two-sex system for her framework. Yet Stefan Hirschauer reminds us that "medical disciplines reconstruct, protect, and mould the life-world distinction between men and women" (13) reinforcing a two-sex dualism and making it salient for rhetorics of health. Within that dualism, Mamo et al. describe the willingness to proscribe interventions for women as "the longstanding medical and cultural pathologization of women's bodies and its concomitant production of their bodies as ripe for medical intervention" (130). Women may be directed to therapies more often than men or pressured to accept treatments that they would not otherwise willingly agree to. Because of the assumptions and attendant pressures, women do not have the same control as men when it comes to health care decisions. In order to understand these distinctions, it helps to understand popularly accepted conceptions of the differences between bodies gendered female and male.

Rhetorics of Health and Medicine in the Literature

Traditionally rhetoricians of health and medicine investigate documents and contexts concerning health care, including medical documents used in hospitals and labs, media attention to health debates, and related documents and discourses. A leading figure in the field, Judy Segal explains that the rhetoric of medicine's "purpose is to assist the understanding of human action in the realm of health and medicine by describing its rhetorical element" (17). Scott et al. expand on Segal's explanation suggesting that "while rhetoricians of health and medicine may not suggest specific corrections to a flawed system, we do, ultimately, believe our work shares some type of ameliorative aim" (3). Within this optimism about amelioration of harm, questions of gender and oppression enter health rhetorics at its outset; in her chapter on migraine headaches, Segal analyzes how gender influences migraine rhetoric to the detriment of female patients (48). Health rhetoric researchers have produced a number of important understandings of health's interaction with gender. From Condit's critique of brain sex research (Condit "How") to Hausman's examination of medical warrants in breastfeeding rhetorics, rhetoricians of health often build from "feminist theorists [that] have long resisted using scientific evidence as an argument for how women should live their lives, because historically most instances of this kind of usage have tried to circumscribe women's freedom with what have come to be understood as fallacious arguments" (Hausman 339). Others approach medicine's attitude toward the gendered body (Shildrik; Grosz) or menstruation (Martin), while Epstein and Owens address pregnancy/childbirth, explaining how "the rhetorical space of the hospital, . . . and the hegemonic nature of Western medicine in the United States, obstructs individual women's abilities to successfully assert agency – as – power in the moments of childbirth" (Owens 1). Owens' attention to removal of agency matches my own concentration on autonomy for women in health settings. Each of these researchers attends to the ways that gender interacts with construction of health and provision of care. As Hausman relates "the concept of rhetorical situation helps us see medical and other types of decision making as they are enacted by socially situated individuals" (332). Using rhetorical tools allow researchers to understand articulated constructions of gendered bodies and illness in the laboratory and in popular culture, and as Scott et al. assert, even hope to amend problems that might arise from those constructions.

Popular Imagery Poses Male Injury Versus Female Cancer

One such construction that presents women's bodies as vulnerable to illness gets repeated in cultural texts. In the enormously popular television show *Lost* the only crash survivor who brings a serious illness to the magical island is Rose Nadler, a middle-aged African-American woman with cancer. While she survives this disease due to the island's healing affects, Rose represents a woman whose body has turned against her.[4] The audience gradually learns she has been diagnosed with terminal cancer in a flashback during season two, but the writers and producers do not reveal the site of her cancer (S.O.S). Another *Lost* character brought by the plane crash, who is also healed by the island, regains use of his legs during the first episode, although viewers are not at first aware of the significance of his ability. John Locke's extraordinary healing circumvents a paralysis below the waist caused by defenestration, which becomes part of his far-fetched narrative. The combination of Nadler's island-cured cancer and Locke's magically reversed paralysis juxtaposes female sickness against male injury from violence, a trope repeated in many contexts.

The imagery of women with cancer becomes laced through much contemporary pop culture, including futuristic worlds where cancer might conceivably be curable or completely eradicated. The science fiction hit

Battlestar Galactica addresses mostly injury rather than illness in the sick bay; the main exception is the breast cancer of President Lara Roslyn. Her ongoing struggle with cancer throughout the series and the cancer's adverse effects on her decision making, become important ways the television show undercuts its own commitment to strong female characters. Roslyn finally succumbs to the disease in the final episode, leaving her male professional counterpart and lover Admiral Adama, who has survived two bullets to the chest, healthy and alone. Both Nadler and Roslyn have aggressive cancers that respond to treatment only in the short term, and each of these otherwise healthy women becomes the only long-term diseased character in their show's artistic universe. Fictional representations of women with cancer are not confined to American television, and these creative narratives build from and add to real-world beliefs about cancer and women.[5] These two award-winning shows enjoin their audiences to suspend their disbelief in extravagantly fictional worlds at least partially because audiences are familiar with women bringing cancerous bodies and men bringing injured bodies into their respective universes.

Those real-world beliefs about potential for illness in female bodies can stem from the laboratory and the clinic. Attitudes about women and cancer originate in older ideas about the inherent weakness and imperfection of women's bodies. Nancy Tuana's book *The Less Noble Sex* affirms how science in Western contexts has long been suffused with negative assumptions about women's nature (biological and temperamental). Tuana traces those ideas from Aristotle through the nineteenth century, explaining that "as we look next at biological theories of woman's nature, we will indeed find that the premise of woman's inherent imperfection has been a fundamental axiom of the biological sciences for centuries" (17). Researchers in the natural and biological sciences historically have built ideas about the weakness of female bodies into their experiments and theories, and these social biases transfer neatly into clinical medicine and public health campaigns. As cultural historian Sander Gilman notes: "cultural differences concerning gender also play a major role in constructing those groups understood as being more at risk" (4). The idea that women's bodies are weak in a number of ways becomes a problem for women who want to use health care services in ways that they control. In her study of gender bias in brain sex research Celeste Condit reminds us that "understanding the social biases we harbor can help us to recognize linguistic biases in research and produce scientific findings less hobbled by linguistic short-comings" ("How" 87). If health care researchers and clinicians begin with inaccurate or only partially accurate assumptions about women's bodies, then they can direct care in inaccurate and inappropriate ways.

Introduction   7

These beliefs about the weakness of the female body extend to cancer predisposition, and cancer itself gets inaccurately viewed as predominantly a woman's disease. Ornella Moscucci's book *Gender and Cancer in England, 1860–1948* explains "it is not exaggeration to say that, in England and in many other Western countries women's cancers have played an outstanding role in positioning cancer in the public domain" (1). Moscucci shows that breast and cervical cancer have long received more attention than other cancer sites. Tammy Duerden Comeau, a researcher in medical sociology, elucidates that "in order to maintain the notion that women were more subject to cancer and that cancer predominantly struck the female breast, 'true' cancer was [originally] deemed to be a hard or scirrhous substance" (Comeau 167). Christa Teston's study of cancer reminds us that "evincing disease is not a solely human enterprise but a matter of rhetorical attunement, in which evidences are coconstructed phenomena" (173). According to Comeau, the need to categorize cancer in a gendered manner convinced nineteenth-century British surgeons to define cancer by its mass rather than using other properties or diagnostic categories as definitional. Comeau's article traces a shift in descriptors for cancer in nineteenth-century British medical texts. Her work further shows how British physicians and researchers were so invested in the gendered nature of cancer that when one gendered representation of cancer was found inaccurate through the advancing of cell theory, "instead of re-considering the reliance on a gendered framework, British surgeons re-incorporated predominant gender ideologies" (Comeau 176). The medical professionals were unable to see beyond their belief that cancer struck women more than men. Beyond the nineteenth century, Leslie Reagan maintains that "women have long been taught that cancer is their special concern and that, indeed, to worry about cancer is their duty" (1779). Yet her conclusion suggests that despite the "dilemmas of targeted health measures: they may be both a necessity and a hazard" (1785). Her work begins to identify in the United States what Moscucci and Comeau have shown in the British context, although she does not go as far as labeling the attitude to women's bodies as oncogenic. My book argues first that such beliefs about cancer as a woman's disease, created in and by female bodies often in their reproductive organs, still inhere in the United States and that those same beliefs are transported to developing nations, like Kenya.

Part of the insistence on cancer as feminine connects to women's capacity in reproduction. Moscucci relays how "the emergence of 'sex' as a category of scientific enquiry gave a different meaning to women's perceived liability to cancer. The rise of gynaecology, the 'science of woman,' legitimated the belief that women's bodies defined their social position and their

8 Introduction

function, which was to reproduce" (15). In their work attending to reproductive technologies, Lay et al. illuminate "how culture tends to define woman according to her reproductive abilities and to divide women's bodies into parts, functions, and processes" (15). If women's bodies can nurture, feed, and protect a group of cells rapidly growing from a fetus to a baby, then certainly their bodies hold the potential to nurture, feed, and protect a group of growing cancerous cells. The assumption that women's bodies inherently produce cancer and may be deemed oncogenic may thus be partially traced to the gestational potential within women's bodies and the assumed similarities between fetuses and cancers as rapidly reproducing cells. Comeau relates the origins of cancer's representation as cell reproduction rather than some other metaphor, arguing that "the portrayal of cancer as reproductive implied that it implicitly belonged in female bodies and reaffirmed cancer as primarily a 'woman's disease'" (175). Jackie Stacey, relying on Julia Kristeva's work on abjection continues the connection between tumor and cancer in her book *Teratologies*, recognizing that "in both states, the body is characterized by a threat of non-differentiation: where does the self end and the other begin?" (91). Stacey explains that "the foetus and the tumour are both constituted by cell growth" (89). The easy transition from reproduction of cells in gestation and the reproduction of cells in cancer make women's bodies, especially their reproductive organs, appear uniquely suited to host cancers.[6] This belief in female weakness, with a focus on cell reproduction in female bodies, bolsters what Celeste Condit labels the genetic model of disease; within "this rhetorical vision, cancer comes not from outside but is, rather, a defect in us, ourselves" (Condit "Women's" 129). Female weakness presenting as genetic failure coupled with imagery of women's bodies as monstrous, what Sarah Alison Miller calls "the medico-philosophical inscription of monstrosity in the female body" (61), and the construction of cancer as cell reproduction allows the biomedical field to construct women's bodies as naturally oncogenic. In this construction, women's bodies passively and almost inevitably create cancer, as if women's bodies are in fact cancer.

In most parts of the world, and under most circumstances, the facts bear out a very different picture than what the oncogenic woman trope implies, as men are just as likely, and sometimes more so, to contract and die from cancer. In fact, the American Cancer Society explains the probability of developing cancer in your lifetime in the United States is 39.6% for men and 37.6% for women, while "risk of dying" is 22% for men and 18.7% for women ("Lifetime Risk"). In a 2011 document titled "Global Cancer Statistics" co-created by the ACS and the International Agency for Research on Cancer (IARC), Ahmedin Jemal et al. provide numbers of estimated new cancer cases and estimated deaths (rather than verified mortality rates) worldwide for all sites but skin.[7] Men account for 6,629,100 new cases and 4,225,700 deaths, while women trail with 6,038,400 new cases and 3,345,800 deaths (Jemal et al. 4). Western Africa (and pockets of Eastern Africa) are the only areas of the globe where cancer mortality is higher for women than for men, which seems connected to their rate of cervical cancer, which stands at 33.7% incidence rate and 24% mortality rate, the second highest in the world. Despite the greater incidence of cancer cases and mortality in men, cultural representations of cancer are still largely gendered female. Moscucci adds "Women's [incorrect] perception of their cancer risk . . .., is not the result of 'ignorance,' but a reflection of the success of policies which, since the early 1900s, have consistently targeted women's cancers a major focus of medical and public health intervention" (1). Those policies elide how the trope of the oncogenic woman rings false statistically and represent a bias about women's bodies within biomedicine and its increasingly globalized culture.

A mixture of unconscious belief in the oncogenic woman couples with the expectation of female responsibility for public health to create a probability that women will attend to cancer screenings and treatments at an early age, regardless of the loss in autonomy engendered by some of these invasive screenings. In her book *Reinventing the Sexes: The Biomedical Construction of Femininity and Masculinity*, Marianne Van Den Wijngaard notes how the idea that women's bodies are inherently different adds to their health care burden. She explains how "focusing on female hormones and application of hormone treatments for a broad range of female diseases sustained and perpetuated ideas and practices in Western culture that were responsible for subjecting females bodies to medical interventions more easily than male bodies" (22). Such biases can manifest in diagnosis and treatment patterns that could remove autonomy from women, much in the ways that women are made responsible for public health outcomes due to their bodily involvement with gestation. In a fascinating manifestation of the oncogenic woman trope, gynecological cancer risk is one of the main reasons that young healthy women in the US see doctors on a regular basis, since they are tasked with papanicolaou tests at ages as young as 18, despite the fact that the highest incidence of cervical cancer occurs between 45 and 64. Despite available vaccines for human papilloma virus, papanicolaou tests to screen for cervical cancer are still recommended for women. These screenings begin for women long before men are suggested to get prostate-specific antigen (PSA) tests or colonoscopies. Indeed men are not even screened for testicular cancer in their early adulthood, despite the knowledge that it strikes younger men.

Attitudes about female responsibility and oncogenic female bodies enter global healthscapes as part of the biomedical incursion of cancer registries, cancer awareness campaigns, and news reports on improvements in cancer treatment, as well as through more explicitly artistic artifacts like novels. In essence, the metaphor of the oncogenic woman easily crosses national borders as part of biomedical incursions and progresses into new, local healthscapes, possibly creating bias for medical practitioners and policy creators against women's bodies and their bodily autonomy. Biomedicine builds gendered understandings of passivity and weakness and susceptibility to cancer into health care methods and treatments, encouraging and enforcing medical interventions for women, while discouraging and ignoring medical interventions for men. This undue burden undercuts two of the four principles of bioethics by removing autonomy from women with the expectation that they will accept medical treatments and interventions for the public good. At the same time, overzealous medical intervention based on gender challenges the bioethical principle of justice, because distribution of responsibility for public health is uneven. Women lose autonomy and men miss the chance for early diagnosis and treatment.

In the 2011 United Nations report titled "Right of Everyone to the Enjoyment of the Highest Attainable Standard of Physical and Mental Health," the rapporteur explains how legal barriers to health care, especially in terms of reproductive care, create inequities in the quality of life and freedoms of people in various contexts. The report suggests that "criminal and other legal restrictions relating to sexual and reproductive health" may have an impact on the right to health recognized by the UN, "in particular on health conditions that only affect women and girls." The focus of the report is on legal and criminal barriers, which the author indicates should be removed by the states that have implemented them. While the report is an important early step toward creating equity in health care access, it places much focus on law and little on the field of health care itself. Legal and cultural barriers to health care are myriad, extensive, intractable, and in some cases growing. However, the increasing globalization of health training, technology, and tools suggest that the medical field itself invites inquiry into the attitudes about women and gendered bodies. These attitudes within the field of biomedicine can add to the barriers for women and flow into attempts at legal and cultural control of women's access to health care. Like legal barriers to reproductive health care, the trope of oncogenic woman gets translated into different settings and affects both medical autonomy of women and access to care for men.

Global Movements of Biomedical Culture

In order to understand those translations of the oncogenic trope, a cultural analyst should study work across the culturescape, including fiction, and medical literature, such as studies of clinical trials, public health documents, and public health policy directives. A combination of scientific, political, and creative artifacts, which all represent the same illness, cancer, together with interview data from health care professionals, can blend a number of disciplinary pieces to build an extended healthscape, or a biomedical culturescape. Using globalism theorist Arjun Appadurai's extension of the term landscape into his five global scapes including mediascapes and financescapes, Adele Clarke creates the term healthscapes "a kind of assemblage, an infrastructure of assumptions as well as people, things, places, images" (401). Appadurai suggests that scapes "are not objectively given relations," instead highlighting "deeply perspectival constructs" (33), and Clarke's description of healthscapes includes images and assumptions. However, healthscapes prioritize biomedical and scientific practices, creating a hierarchy in the artifacts under study. The concept of a culturescape broadens the viewpoint to place disparate texts, including non-biomedical ones, into conversation, retaining Clarke's inclusion of "assumptions." A culturescape extends the Appadurain "perspectival constructs" to ideas and scenes from distant disciplines that can reflect expansive cultural tendencies. Culturescapes allow rhetoricians of medicine to explore an expanded context, thickening researchers' views for more comprehensive analysis of capabilities and global flows.

Reading fiction, media, and policy documents about biomedical situations alongside actual medical documents and interviews with medical professionals displays how the same "assumptions" and gendered ideas from healthscapes also permeate other kinds of cultural products. The fiction about medical events and particular diseases or patients displays similar assumptions in a culturally sanctioned document like a novel. Since novels both reflect and construct culture, they can show how gendered ideas about medicine, disease, or illness builds. In the same way, medical documents, such as research articles, construct the ways medicine will be practiced going forward, so their gender biases can reflect old ideas and push new versions of those ideas into the way we do science and medicine in the future.

Because medicine gets constructed as science (objective and important) despite anthropological and other research that reveals long-standing scientific biases, placing the most scientific of medical literature alongside fiction can show how many of the assumptions built into biomedicine permeate nonscientific culture. This approach of investigating the written documents, both fictional and scientific acknowledges that "even the most seemingly objective medical statement is rhetorical" as Tasha Dubriwny explains (4) and that fiction expands our understanding of medical concepts. Showing just how connected and similar these documents are can accomplish two things. It first displays how fictional narratives build and continue cultural stereotypes both positive and negative that are familiar to science. Additionally, this kind of cultural comparison reveals how deep those cultural stereotypes go. If the same kinds of images and beliefs appear in such different documents, which come from such disparate disciplines, they may need to be studied seriously, addressed, and perhaps dismantled. Investigation of fiction informs the study of gendered cultural beliefs about cancer, partially because cancer already functions as metaphor as well as biomedical reality[8] in clinical settings. The body turning on itself, out of control growth, cells with minds of their own, cells that ignore boundaries, war on the body (or conversely fighting back against the cancer itself) – all of these figurative conceptions of cancer layer it with meaning in excess of prosaic ailments like diabetes or heart disease, despite the potential for metaphor in those illnesses as well. This metaphoric component of cancer creates another justification for using culturescapes, including fiction, to study presuppositions about cancer.

Although this kind of cultural analysis has been done in the genre of science fiction because of its obvious ties to science and technology, other, less clearly connected forms of literature and fiction attend to medical and scientific worlds as well. Building on the hybrid fiction-historical comparison method N. Katherine Hayles develops in *How We Became Posthuman*, this study compares medical and fictional texts and discourses to uncover a cultural network that produces, reproduces, and counters ideas about women's bodies, especially in relation to biomedical practices and public health. In Karla Holloway's important bioethics book *Private Bodies, Public Lives*, she too weaves analysis of fictional texts alongside investigation of medical case studies. She explains how "literary fictions make possible a more complicated life for the legal subject or the medical body than that normally presented in depositions or medical case histories" (10). Of course, scholars like Anne Whitehead move literature and medicine toward the "critical medical humanities, which . . . situate themselves instead in a more critical and analytical relation to medicine" (124). In this model Julia Epstein investigates "medical storytelling . . . from a variety of writings, both medical and literary" to describe "how cultural ideas saturate medical language, [and] how biomedical conceptions of the body put pressure on social ideology" (6). Blending these comparative approaches with Marianne Van Den Wijngaard's feminist critique of scientific and medical writing begins to answer the question of how beliefs, tropes, and warrants create the patterns that impel science. Finally, theorists Saskia Sassen and Arjun Appadurai help describe how Western biomedical beliefs about male and female bodies travel around the world, making access and medical autonomy difficult for women in many contexts. Because global information flows move speedily and soundlessly, separating different types of cultural artifacts from each other to submit them to unrelated analysis no longer works, and global mediations must be studied in tandem. What we believe rather than what we know eventually becomes the facts that speed across the globe.

The Global Mobility of Oncogenic Identities

An investigation of biomedical ideals and their movement across national borders requires an international approach that examines fiction, medical documents, and other human discourses in their disparate global contexts. While Cara Finnegan and Lisa Keränen attend to communicable disease, their call for "a sustained and rigorous analysis of the artifacts, texts, discursive formations, visual representations, and material practices positioned at the nexus of disease and culture" in the context of "anxieties about globalization, identity, and contamination" fits my attention to culture in the study of cancer in its local and global frameworks (225). Scott et al. also recommend that "expanding our purview should also involve heightened attention to transnational rhetorics of health and medicine" (2). Thus, my analysis proceeds through two cases, or culturescapes, from the United States and Kenya. Although the choice to examine two spaces – the United States and Kenya – may seem an unlikely one, there are a number of historical similarities that make the comparison useful. Additionally, cultural and economic disparities heighten the significances of medical and scientific correspondence. The influence of globalism, especially Western biomedicalization, links the two locations of the United States and Kenya. As Clarke et al. maintain, "western medicines . . . have been traveling widely for many centuries, especially but not only through imperial colonial and post-colonial projects" (31). Each of these countries was colonized by England at some point, suggesting that cultural flows became a reality long ago. Finally, they are both majority Christian nations, with Protestantism of all denominations the most prevalent and Catholicism second.

Despite similarities in postcolonial status and religion, which permit a comparison, these countries represent distinct cultures with differing levels of development, and their differences allow inquiry into the pervasiveness and the effects of biomedicine's global reach. Most obviously, researchers and clinicians in the wealthy United States represent one of the main sources of biomedicine. Despite some changes in spending patterns that shift research to Asia (Chakma et al.), much medical research still originates in the relatively wealthy US. Consequently, one could expect to find biomedical assumptions and methods throughout the US system, a huge medical infrastructure with myriad hospitals, private clinics, independent doctor's practices, and other facilities. Contrasting with the US primacy in the biomedical industry, investigating Kenya allows a window into a hybrid health system with both biomedical and traditional healers represented to varying degrees. Kenya's biomedical infrastructure is newer and less complex than the United States. While displaying some amazing successes, Kenya remains a developing country with many of the social challenges of the region, including unemployment, political instability, and intra-group violence. Its medical system comprises both traditional medicine and Western biomedicine, but some Kenyans have little access to health care of any kind. In fact, cancer care infrastructures in Kenya builds directly from North American and Western sources, notably with assistance from the International Agency for Research on Cancer (IARC), which along with the World Health Organization aided Drs. Anne Korir and Geoffrey Mutuma and Mr. Nathan Okerosi in developing the Nairobi Cancer Registry. Importantly, Mutuma first visited the National Cancer Institutes in Washington DC to train for cancer registry work. These two countries from North America and Africa, diverse continents, integrate Western biomedicine to different degrees. Yet, in each of these different, albeit connected, settings, the biomedical influence is comprehensive enough to be studied for the effects of its integration on gender and cancer care.

In the final chapter of *Biomedicalization: Technoscience, Health, and Illness in the U.S.*, Adele Clark calls for a global and transnational analysis of biomedicalization and the ethical issues imbedded therein. Her chapter points to complicating factors like postcolonialism, neocolonialism, and the troubled links between biomedicalization and public health, as well as the difficulty in even settling upon definitions for Western medicine itself. Responding to that call from Clarke requires bringing together different types of documents from these various developed and developing settings to investigate how gendered identities are constructed from medical documents and the culture of Western medicine that builds from and around those documents. Forms such as research articles and cancer registries reflect common patterns in biomedicine. Globalism theorist and sociologist Saskia Sassen suggests that new patterns and forms, such as the move away from the nation-state during globalism, always contain some of the previous patterns, and that the seeds of the current changes exist in previous times. She goes on to explain "that such capabilities are collective productions whose development requires time . . . they are constitutive of assemblages, even as the latter in turn produce organizing logics that reposition those capabilities" (13). Like the shift to globalized structures that contain relics of nation-states, global health initiatives contain capabilities that may be repositioned in new settings like Kenya, but also maintain the residue of their origins. While invested in progressive ideals and new global allowances, these initiatives exist in Western medical ways of thinking.

Such biomedicalized accepted wisdom infilitrates local and national health care situations. In addition to progressive ideals, globalization of biomedicine can carry entrenched biases about gendered bodies. Sassen builds on what economist Amartya Sen and political philosopher Martha Nussbaum call a "capability." Saskia Sassen explains that "a given capability can contribute to the formation of a very different relational system from the one it originates in" (8). She argues that "the critical issue is the intermediation that capabilities produce between the old and the new orders: as they jump tracks they are in part constitutive and at the same time can veil the switch by wearing some of the same old clothes" (8). The capability of global medicine transcends national boundaries and ignores local medical traditions because of an authority developed in the nineteenth and twentieth centuries. Western biomedicalization becomes a capability that may "wear the clothes" of ancient attitudes about women's weakness and unfit bodies, while simultaneously bringing progress and medical opportunity. Because the biomedical field usually brings with it physicians and other medical practitioners, pharmaceuticals, equipment, and even facilities, it gets welcomed, although not wholly uncritically, in transnational settings. If research and development in biomedicine did not flow from the US to countries like Kenya, then diseases like HIV-AIDS would be almost untreatable. The medicines and skills transfer from developed to developing world could be recognized as a global success. Yet, the underlying disempowering assumptions about women's different bodies that predate, form, and permeate science and medicine can seep into those transfers, carrying damaging thought patterns and behaviors from the West to the developing countries. Despite some critique of Western practices and belief structures from traditional medicine and from local biomedical researchers, this phenomenon creates a fertile ground for unquestioning acceptance of biases imbedded within the medical field. Novels and medical journals, Texas policy documents and gubernatorial statements, CDC sponsored clinical trials, and Kenyan public health organizations all reflect the culture of Western biomedicine, providing spaces to investigate whether, and how, such biases move into new spaces as well. The interview data especially reveals Kenyan health care professionals replicating the epistemological frames they have learned in biomedical training.

The second chapter provides a model for reading the culturescape for oncogenic tropes, by investigating the complex interactions between biomedical research, marketing campaigns, popular coverage of medical research, and fiction, all creating beliefs and practices around women's bodies. I trace those beliefs through research on efficacy of mammograms to show how machines and networks gain agency as women lose it. I locate it in advertising contexts, where pink ribbons festooned upon commercial products provide women with constant reminders that their bodies have the ability to produce deviant cells and in *Good Harbor*, a novel of friendship between women. In Texas, rhetorical progression from scientific documents to media representations in their initial vaccination recommendations for the Gardasil vaccine crafts particular identity formations and attaches notions of risk to created categories of people, in particular women and girls. The chapter offers a contextual framework for the Kenya examples that follow; it provides a way to understand how the oncogenic women impression operates in various situations.

Chapter 3 makes Kenya the focus and argues that cancer's causes become constructed differently based upon the gender of the sufferer, building upon the inevitability of cancer in women to reinforce passive acquisition of cancer for women's bodies. Using analysis of Kenyan author Margaret Ogola's final novel, *Place of Destiny*, wherein two characters die of very different cancers, I unearth gendered representation of the disease. Ogola's status as both Kenyan writer and medical practitioner provides a direct example of biomedical influence on nonscientific cultural production and conversely cultural influence on biomedical practitioners. The text insists that the female character's liver cancer is passively acquired, while the male character's nose and throat cancer results from his choice to smoke. This representation of passive female bodies that naturally contract cancer subtly supports enforced bodily passivity and reduction in bodily autonomy for women.

For Chapter 4, the investigation of the Kenyan context expands into medical and policy documents. I argue that global transference of Western biomedical technologies and practices are both propitious and disciplinary. Comparing reports from two cancer registries – the Nairobi Cancer Registry (NCR), hosted at the Kenya Medical Research Institute (KEMRI), and the Eldoret Cancer Registry – as well as a cancer policy document from the Kenyan Parliament, demonstrates the path of biomedical practices into Kenya and its health systems. These documents and the Kenyan history of integrating cancer technologies follow the gendered path Moscucci describes, and they display – at varying levels – familiar tropes like oncogenic women and a willingness to prescribe both behavioral and medical interventions on women's bodies, as well as the hesitation to prescribe behavioral or medical interventions on men's bodies.

Chapter 5 adds data collected from Kenyan health care professionals during 2016 and 2017. In this chapter, I present evidence from biomedical practitioners in Kenya engaging in familiar attitudes about cancer in women, and share their additional insights that could be useful for Kenyan cancer care going forward. The interview data includes answers to questions like who suffers from cancer the most: men or women, which complement and complicate the fictional representation of cancer in male and female bodies and the constructions of cancer in medical and policy documents.

Sharpening the focus on globalism as transmitter of cultural inequities, especially medical ideas about gender, shows how biomedicine can visit procedures on unwilling bodies or refuse care to the wrong types of bodies. The bioethical justice principal exposes problems of access based on location, class, race, and gender, and is further complicated by the notion of ability to refuse care. Justice implies both a potential for additional access to treatments and care and an increasing recognition of personal autonomy. If implemented, this justice principle would bolster women's ability to deny or eschew medical interventions, despite public health concerns or even legal responsibilities that burden them with medical expectations. Globalism is meant to improve access to health care by communicating health care techniques, pharmaceuticals, and providers around the globe, but additionally it often carries the imbedded assumptions about health care and bodies, thereby increasing inequities in the health care system. The same assumptions about female bodies, which manifest in fiction and medical documents around the world, demand a contravening push for justice and autonomy. An intervention into this transmission of gendered ideals accompanied with careful investigation of gender imbalance could create better access to health care, sustain more ability to make autonomous health care decisions, and allow patients to refuse care when necessary for their personal well-being.

Notes

1. For full treatment, see Rosumund Scott *Rights, Duties and the Body*.
2. Fuller treatment in Julia Epstein's chapter "Dangerous Wombs." See also the National Women's Law Center.
3. The initial UK vaccination plan (1970–1988) only vaccinated female children (Tookey 2004) not because the burden of disease for rubella fell on women but because the burden of disease fell on fetuses in the form of congenital rubella syndrome (CRS).
4. Rose's portrayal as wise and mystic black woman could bear additional scrutiny.
5. See Chapter 1 for cancer narratives and fiction. See also Goodreads www.goodreads.com/shelf/show/breast-cancer for a list of Popular Breast Cancer Books.
6. Indeed rare cancers, called gestational trophoblastic disease, develop from placental cells, which normally reproduce rapidly to become the fetus's food; in GTD, these cells proliferate into cancer. Such cancers are rare, and could not account for the attitudes linking cancer to women's bodies.
7. Using "All sites but skin" totals is common in cancer registries. In cancer research and publications, "sites" refer to the part of the body, usually a particular organ, where the cancer manifests, with the primary site being where the cancer first appears.
8. See Richard T. Penson et al.'s "Cancer as Metaphor."

Works Cited

Appadurai, Arjun. *Modernity at Large: Cultural Dimensions of Globalization*. U of Minnesota P, 1996.

Chakma, Justin et al. "Asia's Ascent – Global Trends in Biomedical R&D Expenditures." *The New England Journal of Medicine*, vol. 370, no. 1, 2014, pp. 3–6.

Clarke, Adele. "Thoughts on Biomedicalization and Its Transnational Travels." *Biomedicalization: Technoscience, Health, and Illness in the U.S.*, edited by Adele Clarke, Duke UP, 2010, pp. 380–405.

Clarke, Adele et al. *Biomedicalization: Technoscience, Health, and Illness in the U.S.* Duke UP, 2010.

Comeau, Tammy Duerden. "Gender Ideology and Disease Theory: Classifying Cancer in Nineteenth Century Britain." *Journal of Historical Sociology*, vol. 20, nos. 1–2, 2007, pp. 158–81.

Condit, Celeste. "How Bad Science Stays That Way: Brain Sex, Demarcation, and the Status of Truth in the Rhetoric of Science." *Rhetoric Society Quarterly*, vol. 26, no. 4, 1996, pp. 83–109.

———. "Women's Reproductive Choices and the Genetic Model of Medicine." *Body Talk: Rhetoric, Technology, Reproduction*, edited by Mary M. Lay et al., U of Wisconsin P, 2000, pp. 125–40.

Diamant, Anita. *Good Harbor*. Scribner, 2002.

Dubriwny, Tasha N. *The Vulnerable Empowered Woman*. Rutgers UP, 2013.

Epstein, Julia. *Altered Conditions: Disease, Medicine, and Storytelling*. Routledge, 1995.

Finnegan, Cara A., and Lisa Keränen. "Review Essay: Addressing the Epidemic of Epidemics: Germs, Security, and a Call for Biocriticism." *Quarterly Journal of Speech*, vol. 97, no. 2, 2011, pp. 224–44.

Foucault, Michel. *The History of Sexuality*. 1st American ed. Pantheon, 1978.

Gilman, Sander L. *Disease and Representation: Images of Illness from Madness to AIDS*. Cornell UP, 1988.

Grosz, E.A. *Volatile Bodies: Toward a Corporeal Feminism*. Indiana UP, 1994.

Hausman, Bernice L. "Breastfeeding, Rhetoric, and the Politics of Feminism." *Journal of Women, Politics & Policy*, vol. 34, no. 4, 2013, pp. 330–44.

Hayles, N. Katherine. *How We Became Posthuman: Virtual Bodies in Cybernetics, Literature, and Informatics*. U of Chicago P, 1999.

Hirschauer, Stefan. "Performing Sexes and Genders in Medical Practices." *Differences in Medicine: Unravelling Practices, Techniques, and Bodies*, edited by Marc Berg and Annemarie Mol, Duke UP, 1998, pp. 13–27.

Holloway, Karla. *Private Bodies, Public Texts: Race, Gender, and a Cultural Bioethics*. Duke UP, 2011.

Jemal, Ahmedin et al. "Global Cancer Statistics." *CA: A Cancer Journal for Clinician*, vol. 61, no. 2, 2011, pp. 69–90.

Lay, Mary M. et al. *Body Talk: Rhetoric, Technology, Reproduction*. U of Wisconsin P, 2000.

Lieber, Jeffrey, J.J. Abrams, and Damon Lindelof, creators. *Lost*. Bad Robot Production and ABC Studios, 2010.

"Lifetime Risk of Developing or Dying of Cancer." American Cancer Society (ACS), www.cancer.org/cancer/cancer-basics/lifetime-probability-of-developing- or-dying-from-cancer.html

Mamo, Laura, Amber Nelson, and Aleia Clark. "Producing and Protecting Risky Girlhoods." *Three Shots at Prevention: The HPV Vaccine and the Politics of Medicine's Simple Solutions,* edited by Keith Wailoo et al., The Johns Hopkins UP, 2010, pp. 121–45.

Martin, E. "Medical Metaphors of Women's Bodies: Menstruation and Menopause." *International Journal of Health Services*, vol. 18, 1988, pp. 237–54.

Miller, Sarah Alison. *Medieval Monstrosity and the Female Body.* Routledge, 2010.

Moore, Ronald D., creator. *Battlestar Gallactica.* David Eick Productions and NBC Universal Television Studio, 2004.

Moscucci, Ornella. *Gender and Cancer in England, 1860–1948.* Palgrave, 2016.

Ogola, Margaret. *Place of Destiny.* Paulines Publication Africa, 2005.

Owens, Kim H. *Writing Childbirth: Women's Rhetorical Agency in Labor and Online.* Southern Illinois UP, 2015.

Penson, Richard T. et al. "Cancer as Metaphor." *The Oncologist,* vol. 9, no. 6, 2004, pp. 708–16.

Reagan, Leslie J. "Engendering the Dread Disease: Women, Men and Cancer." *American Journal of Public Health,* vol. 87 no. 11, 1997, pp. 1779–86.

Sassen, Saskia. *Territory Authority Rights: From Medieval to Global Assemblages.* Princeton UP, 2006.

Scott, J. Blake. *Risky Rhetoric: Aids and the Cultural Practices of HIV Testing.* Southern Illinois UP, 2003.

Scott, J. Blake et al. "The Rhetorics of Health and Medicine: Inventional Possibilities for Scholarship and Engaged Practice." *Poroi: An Interdisciplinary Journal of Rhetorical Analysis & Invention,* vol. 9, no. 1, 2013, pp. 2–9.

Scott, Rosumund. *Rights, Duties and the Body: Law and Ethics of the Maternal-Fetal Conflict.* Hart Publishing, 2002.

Segal, Judy Z. *Health and the Rhetoric of Medicine.* Southern Illinois UP, 2008.

Shildrik, M. *Leaky Bodies: Feminism, Postmodernism, and (Bio)ethics.* Routledge, 1997.

"S.O.S." *Lost: Season 2.* Written by Steven Maeda & Leonard Dick, directed by Eric Laneuville, ABC Network, 2006.

Stacey, Jackie. *Teratologies: A Cultural Study of Cancer.* Routledge, 1999.

Teston, Christa. *Bodies in Flux: Scientific Methods for Negotiating Medical Uncertainty.* U of Chicago P, 2017.

Tookey, P. "Rubella in England, Scotland and Wales." *Euro Surveillance: Bulletin European Sur Les Maladies Transmissibles = European Communicable Disease Bulletin,* vol. 9, no. 4, 2004, pp. 21–23.

Tuana, Nancy. *The Less Noble Sex: Scientific, Religious, and Philosophical Conceptions of Woman's Nature.* Indiana UP, 1993.

United Nations Special Rapporteur. *Human Rights Council.* Right of Everyone to the Enjoyment of the Highest Attainable Standard of Physical and Mental Health, 2011.

Whitehead, Anne. "The Medical Humanities: A Literary Perspective Overview." *Medicine, Health and the Arts: Approaches to the Medical Humanities*, edited by Victoria Bates et al., Routledge, 2014, pp. 107–27.

Wijngaard, Marianne van den. *Reinventing the Sexes: The Biomedical Construction of Femininity and Masculinity*. Indiana UP, 1997.

2 Oncogenic Women in a Cancer Culturescape

The culturescape of cancer in the US and beyond reflects gendering of cancer that has been identified in early cancer research (Comeau) as well as cancer programs in the US and England (Moscucci). Two types of female reproductive cancers, breast and cervical, remain the face of cancer fears in the twenty-first century, and cancer anxieties deploy to discipline female bodies and limit bodily agency for women and people with breasts and cervixes. Comparative cultural inattention to non-gendered cancers like liver and colorectal cancers, not to mention reticence to screen for prostate cancer,[1] which is gendered male, means that men retain almost complete agency over their bodies and health care decisions – a result of social power maintained in clinical settings. Yet the silence around male cancer may also facilitate negative material realities like ineffective screening or later stage diagnosis. For women, fear of cancer becomes an effective maintenance of discipline, convincing them to distrust their own bodies and trust biomedical technologies and practices. Older fears about pregnancy and women's uncontrollable sexuality traditionally used to solidify gender hierarchies and contain female power get redeployed as fear of breast cancer and cervical cancer – cast as sexually transmitted disease – often compelling women to present their bodies for screenings and vaccinations. As Foucault reminds us "the medical examination" acts as a "mechanism . . . exercising a power that questions, monitors, watches, spies, searches out, palpates, brings to light" (45). Unevenly distributed information about cancer incidence, mortality, screening, and treatment coalesce with situated discourses of fear to complicate agency for gendered actors. Thus, health care decision making remains available, if distorted, to men and removed from women.

This cancer culturescape model derives from Arjun Appadurai's global scapes in *Modernity at Large*. Appadurai foregrounds the term "concatenation" to describe his scapes and foregrounds that they are "not objectively given relations" (33) but rather combinations that might at first seem disjointed. This concept of concatenation, strings or chains of things depending upon one another, underpins culturescapes. By bringing together seemingly disparate cultural artifacts, both biomedical, policy, popular, and high culture, which depend upon one another to erect a cultural understanding of cancer, researchers can assemble and investigate that larger understanding both as a biomedical reality and also as a cultural marker that exceeds the boundaries of medicine. Appadurai's scapes represent "dimensions of global cultural flows" (33) meant to join economic globalization and international capital movement with their cultural dimensions. My construction of culturescapes might be read as an attempt to re-nationalize global flows, as I describe them in somewhat national frameworks from America and Kenya; however, I see it as description of localized, contextual expression of those global currents. The Komen Foundation's role in the culturescape provides a useful example as Komen relies on bodily hierarchies that predate the United States. The Komen Foundation was founded during the 1980s in the US, and since 2013 maintains international presence with Special Consultative Status with the United Nations Economic and Social Council (ECOSOC), spreading pinkification to the international community. Its effects are situated locally, nationally, and internationally, while postage stamps and CDC recommendations are issued at the national level.

Novelistic Breast Cancer Fears

Understanding the culturescape of cancer thus requires attention to medical, fictional, and popular artifacts that constitute information and attitudes about cancer. Because so many types of biomedical and cultural production swirl in this culturescape, a composite of the concatenation becomes useful. A concatenation of persuasion about female embodiment, particularly breasts and cervixes as inexorably cancer producing or oncogenic includes biomedical research and ensuing popular debate about mammography efficacy, because mammograms have become a cipher for early detection in cancer care, as well as a materially embedded process through which we discipline female bodies. To bridge biomedical sources and fictions that reach a broader audience, an analysis of *Good Harbor*, the second novel by best-selling author Anita Diamant and its reification of breast cancer fears reveals how "literary fictions make possible a more complicated life for the legal subject or the medical body than that normally presented in depositions of medical case histories" (Holloway 10). Finally, a cancer culturescape includes analysis from the introduction of Gardasil to the American health topography, which reflects women's assumed oncogenic nature when early biomedical inquiry, marketing efforts, and political policy directed the vaccine toward girls and women, while perpetrating a somewhat dangerous exclusion of boys and men.

In 2016, breast cancer incurred the largest number of new cases for women in the United States with 246,660 of the total 843,820 new cancer cases in women, making it a legitimate health concern (Cancer Facts). Yet both lung cancer and cancers of the digestive system outpace breast cancer for number of deaths in women for 2016 (Cancer Facts). Despite morbidity information, vast networks of breast cancer marketing include consumer products connected to cancer research through charitable organizations, as well as public health campaigns to encourage mammograms, and literature themed on breast cancer tragedies and victories. In that vein, a number of novels, poems, essays, and other works, including television shows, highlight incidence of breast cancer.[2] A few famous breast cancer novels include Margaret Atwood's *Bodily Harm*, Karin Cook's *What Girls Learn*, and Mary Alice Monroe's *Time is a River*. For nonfiction narratives, Judy Segal's "Breast Cancer Narratives as Public Rhetoric" performs an analysis of predominantly first-person narratives of breast cancer. While some examples of male cancer narrative exist, such as Walter White's non-gendered lung cancer diagnosis, there does not appear to be an entire sub-genre of prostate cancer novels or colon cancer diaries.[3] Some marketing efforts do exist to remind men that their bodies also have the capacity for cancer, such as growing mustaches in November, to encourage getting prostate exams and raise money for research. Yet these campaigns pale in comparison to breast cancer awareness products and chronicles. In fact, efforts to increase awareness, which earlier had been useful, show that Americans are quite aware of the breast cancer risk. Yadlon suggests that "breast cancer discourse not only emerges from ideological assumptions but performs cultural work" (647) and "produces a particular kind of gendered guilt" connected to procreative and nutritive choices coded female (648). Increasingly, efforts within health care contexts and surrounding milieus have effectively created attentiveness that subtly influences beliefs about cancer, re-deploying tropes about female bodies, particularly their reproductive organs, as oncogenic.

A number of efforts to contribute to breast cancer research build from and into this oncogenic narrative, building fear rhetoric into their appeals. Laurie Selleck reports that in 2003 "breast cancer is the health threat about which women are most aware" (122). Women may be aware that heart disease remains both more prevalent and more deadly, but the fear of developing breast cancer also connects to aging and appearance, gendered concerns that reinforce difference in women's bodies. Selleck addresses the Susan Komen Foundation strategy of putting ribbons on "products designed to remind them of . . . threat" (Selleck 119). The immense campaign to convince American consumers to buy products that donate proceeds to breast cancer research, called pinkwashing by Samantha King and decried by others,[4] both participates in and contributes to Western ideas about cancer and women's bodies. Tapping into long-standing beliefs that women are especially prone to all disease and cancer in particular, the Komen Foundation reinforces women's extant anxiety, partially through implementation of the pink ribbon imagery employing a color that American culture associates with women.[5] The result for the collective imaginings of millions of women is that breast cancer is omnipresent, and fear that their bodies will inevitably turn on them and produce malignant, redundant cells.

To create a fuller picture of the culturescape for cancer, examining fictional representations of breast cancer complements the view of Komen efforts. Holloway explains how fictional texts "reveal the deeply textured terrains in which stories (or cases) reside" (10), and how such analysis adds to the traditional artifacts studied by rhetoricians of medicine. Anita Diamant's novel *Good Harbor* reflects and (re)produces attitudes toward breast cancer in American culture. One of its two protagonists, Kathleen, follows a familiar narrative of cancer diagnosis and treatment. A returning trope for Kathleen's character represents friends and acquaintances who approach her with their own breast cancer stories. The protagonist encounters reflexive cancer chronicles again and again, when characters inevitably refer to a friend or relative who had contracted breast cancer. Early in the novel Kathleen relates one such history when, "Madge shook her head sadly, sighed, and said, 'You know, my ma had it too'" (25). She grows weary of hearing about other victims as people volunteer solidarity without being asked. The compulsively repeated practice becomes something of a joke to Kathleen as she "heard that refrain again and again. Like a parade of cats with dead mice in their teeth, five teachers, two aides, and a lunch lady came to the library and laid the tale of the mother's, sister's, best friend's breast cancer at her feet. As though she didn't have Pat's story, her own sister" (Diamant 25). The annoyance and dark humor of Kathleen's character aside, this trope reinforces the ubiquity of breast cancer, fueling extant fears of the disease. Emphasizing breast cancer as a major plot line normalizes the disease – a boon for actual survivors, who can feel marginalized or underserved by our culture's relentless focus on health and fitness. Yet this same normalization persuades readers that breast cancer awaits healthy women regardless of genetics, behaviors, exposure to toxins, or luck, embedding the novel in rhetorics of bodily hierarchy and material disciplinarity.

The novel also refers to the extant fear of breast cancer that its own rhetoric encourages revealing how "literary fictions reveal their embeddedness in our cultural and aesthetic traditions" (Holloway 66). The inescapability of disease incites a fear response so that "Kathleen knew why she hadn't called: too many friends and family members had been diagnosed with cancer in the past few years, and Jeanette was terrified" (69). The protagonist uses alarming language to describe her friend's emotions and her reason for avoiding the protagonist. Of course, humans often respond to illness with fear, but Kathleen connects the prevalence of cancer in their friend group with the term "terrified." With this shorthand, the novel reinforces both the conception that breast cancer is preordained invoking "too many friends," who had succumbed, and reinforces terror as an appropriate response to the concept of breast cancer.

The novel itself fortifies the narrative of oncogenic women and critical treatment of it repeats that refrain. One review of Good Harbor on the *Curled up with a Good Book* website reifies the claim that breast cancer is ubiquitous. While praising the novel, this reviewer suggests that "the story is universal. Both women deal with their inner emotional and spiritual lives as all women do: the aging and healing processes, coping with marital bliss and stress, and the life changes of children" (Chopra). The words "universal," and "all women" coupled with a subsequent assertion that issues of "breast cancer and the empty-nest syndrome, are ones that middle-aged women face" buttress the inevitability of breast cancer that the novel itself portrays (Chopra). While an online review for a popular novel cannot exchange for medical advice, these kinds of cultural production weave into a constructed narrative about breast cancer's prevalence and the supposed oncogenic nature of women's bodies.

Broader Culture Replays Breast Cancer Fears

Beyond Komen pink marketing, fundraising, and fictional cancer narratives, other cultural markers reflect the outsize attention to breast cancer in American culture. In 1998, the postal service issued a breast cancer postage stamp, which allowed donation from survivors and friends. This breast cancer stamp was the inaugural *semipostal* stamp, allowing "revenue from sales . . . to be transferred to a selected executive agency or agencies" allowing fundraising for entities outside the postal service itself for the first time (USPS Semipostal) (Figure 2.1). A 33 cent prostate cancer awareness stamp was issued in 1999, as well as three other cancer-related stamps: the earliest cancer stamp, a non-gendered crusade against cancer commemorative five cent stamp issued in 1965, the 1978 13 cent stamp honoring Dr. George Papanicolaou, who developed cervical cancer screening, and an earlier breast cancer awareness 32 cent stamp issued in 1996 complete with a pink ribbon (National). As another reflection of oncogenic discourse, the majority of US postal stamps associated with cancer concern women's reproductive organs, and no colon, skin, or lung cancer stamp has been issued at this time. The existence of two breast cancer stamps and pink

Figure 2.1 Breast cancer semipostal stamp
Credit: Miriam O'Kane Mara

ribbons festooned upon all forms of commercial goods invoke persistent reminders that women's othered bodies have the innate ability to produce deviant reproducing cells. Those discursive signals in the culturescape permeate messaging about the likely risk for breast and other gendered cancers. Very few other health campaigns worked so deeply into the cultural consciousness.

This reflection of oncogenic bodies coupled with a cultural imperative toward women's duty toward public health complicate women's ability to choose or refuse procedures in clinical settings. Blake Scott's investigation of HIV testing shows "how testing and its rhetorics function as disciplinary mechanisms of power . . . influenced by those of other prevention efforts and biomedicine" (36). Like HIV testing, in mammography discourse, even as various sources buttress oncogenic messaging, women are encouraged to offer their bodies for screenings like mammogram under the aegis of *prevention*. Jennifer Fosket reminds us that biomedical efforts like mammogram "detect" cancer rather than preventing it, highlighting the rhetorical slippage in biomedical discourse attending to cancer screening (335). Thus detection seeps into prevention narratives, blurring the very concept of prevention. The vernacular of prevention itself requires consideration, as increasing attention paid to preventive care in Western biomedicine works against the very concept of bodily autonomy by recommending procedures, like mammogram, *before* patients present with illness.[6] This kind of early intervention, while perhaps efficacious in finding disease, surely does not prevent it, and may in fact find disease that needs no treatment.[7] In fact, new mammogram research in 2014 suggests severe limitations in the efficacy of the procedure, especially at earlier ages. Yet, patterns of representation in medicine, popular culture, and media provide agency to what Bruno Latour calls [non-human] actants like mammogram machines as well as health care professionals, while removing agency from other actors, individual female embodied persons especially (54). The national cancer institute fact sheet on mammograms explains that "the x-ray images make it possible to detect tumors that cannot be felt" (Mammograms). The implication is that the human touch falls short of adequate cancer finding agency here; rather, a machine and digital image perform better screening and diagnosis. Such innocuous information about the efficacy of mammogram machines and the images they produce become part of the network of health care and imbue those tools with agential power that the women circulated through those networks are denied. A conversation that grants more agency to the tools used in health care setting than to the potential patients, drains autonomy from women and situates their bodies as sites of intervention and investigation through recommended or required screenings.

Yet, research shows that this omnipresent tool in the breast cancer arsenal, mammography, is not the panacea it was billed, and suggests breast cancer is overdiagnosed. A February 2014 article for *British Medical Journal* titled "Twenty Five Year Follow-Up for Breast Cancer Incidence and Mortality of the Canadian National Breast Screening Study" by Miller et al. concludes that: "in technically advanced countries, our results support the views of some commentators that the rationale for screening by mammography should be urgently reassessed by policy makers" (5). They add "our data show that annual mammography **does not** result in a reduction in breast cancer specific mortality for women aged 40–59 beyond that of physical examination alone or usual care in the community" (5). While the authors underscore the importance of mammography for older women, they stress that one of the reasons for rethinking mammograms for younger women is overdiagnosis.

Overdiagnosis here refers to the possibility that a mammography detected cancer might not otherwise become clinically apparent during the lifetime of the woman. An April 2014 *Journal of American Medical Association* (*JAMA*) article also suggests mammograms for younger women were less efficacious and that decisions be based on personal risk (Pace and Keating). A February 2014 article in the *New England Journal of Medicine* by Swiss Medical Board members, extends the *BMJ* and *JAMA* study findings. Authors explain that "44,925 healthy women in the screening group were diagnosed with and treated for breast cancer *unnecessarily*, which resulted in needless surgical interventions, radiotherapy, chemotherapy, or some combination of these therapies" (Biller-Andorno et al. 1965, my emphasis). These numbers convince the writers that such negative outcomes may be more important than the benefits accrued from regularized mammography screenings. They go on to lament "the pronounced discrepancy between women's perceptions of the benefits of mammography screening and the benefits to be expected in reality" (1966). The researchers finally suggest providing women more accurate information:

> The majority of women believe that it prevents or reduces the risk of getting breast cancer and saves many lives through early detection of aggressive tumors.[4] We would be in favor of mammography screening if these beliefs were valid. Unfortunately, they are not, and we believe that women need to be told so. From an ethical perspective, a public health program that does not clearly produce more benefits than harms is hard to justify. Providing clear, unbiased information, promoting appropriate care, and preventing overdiagnosis and overtreatment would be a better choice.
>
> (Biller-Adorno 1967)

Their focus on placing more evidence and data into women's hands matches the ethic of autonomy and maintains the other ethical principles of non-maleficence, beneficence, and justice. This board suggests providing women with additional data and stepping back from restrictive, non-nuanced recommendations for mammography. However, these Swiss Medical Board officials may reflect more attention to autonomy than American health professionals, who value patient compliance. Their findings that women's beliefs about benefit differ considerably from actual benefit reflect the cultural tendency to persuade women that medical intervention can prevent impending negative health outcomes, persuasion that depends upon a background terror of breast cancer. In other words, women are convinced that mammography can banish such terror. Overdiagnosis has not been imbued with the same dread, and thus does not prevent women from seeking unnecessary procedures, despite it being the very source of much of the terror it seeks to alleviate.

The Swiss board suggests that mammography might prevent one death for every 1000 women screened, but that in comparison "490 to 670 women are likely to have a false positive mammogram with repeat examination; 70 to 100, an unnecessary biopsy; and 3 to 14, an overdiagnosed breast cancer that would never have become clinically apparent" (Biller-Adorno 1966). The number of harms from mammography ranges from the top end of 490 false positives, which itself creates stress and often sends women for more testing. While false positives are the least harmful, the numbers are high. If one merely compares the lowest end of the possible harms, overdiagnoses, three is higher than the one death, which might be prevented. Despite such numbers, many cancer experts are loathe to abandon mammography screening for younger women. Medical professionals and the general public tend to recognize the benefits of medical care: screenings, pharmaceuticals, procedures. They find it more difficult to integrate the iatrogenic effects (or harms) of care, such as overdiagnosis.

In the face of those findings, the United States Preventive Services Task Force (USPSTF) changed their recommendations in April 2015 to suggest regular mammogram for women 50–75, while giving a C recommendation for women 40–49. They explain "a C recommendation for this age group isn't a recommendation against mammography but instead means the USPSTF sees only a small net benefit" (USPSTF Still Recommends). Contrarily, the American Cancer Society and the Mayo Clinic both refused to shift and "reaffirm that screening mammography for women in their 40s is associated with a decrease in breast cancer deaths" (Douda). Emphasis on "breast cancer deaths" keeps fear of women's oncogenic nature in the foreground and maintains earlier screening of female bodies, undercutting agency and autonomy for persons gendered female. This kind of enthusiasm for screening women in the face of research that shows actual harm does not hold for male screenings.[8]

Media coverage about the medical findings about iatrogenic effects from mammogram in 2014 and 2015 builds upon the fear that Selleck identifies. Reporting from four large newspapers suggests that most media outlets seem unwilling to make negative statements about medical tests for women, especially when they could fulfill a promise of early detection. While mainstream publications like *USA Today*, and the *Washington Post* covered the groundbreaking studies from the *British Medical Journal* and the article in *JAMA*, they mostly do **not** cover the *NEJM* Swiss board article, although Forbes and NY Times did. Some of the articles justified mammogram and made smoothing efforts to downplay the new research in their reporting.

A more in-depth investigation of one article, Lennie Bernstein's piece in the *Washington Post*, displays those tendencies to modulate critique of mammogram technologies and practices. He begins: "Mammography's benefits are substantial, but its potential harms may be greater than previously realized" (Bernstein). The story leads with a strong independent clause of only four words; the strong adjective "substantial" connects with a *to be* verb to the nouns "Mammography's benefits," with no qualifying adverbs. This short, persuasive clause makes an easy to read and understand claim. The dependent clause that follows connects a pronoun pointing back to mammography, rather than the word itself, with "harms," modified and qualified by "potential" with a compound version of the *to be* verb including "may" rather than the stronger verb – are – of the first clause. All of the qualifying words make the dependent claim even weaker and more difficult to process. To muddy the clause further, using "its" rather than mammography's in front of harms blurs what might cause those "potential harms." The term mammography recurs five times in this article, three times it occurs close to the word benefit, although it is closer to the word risk in one of those three occasions. The final use pairs "mammography" with neither benefit nor harm, nor even risk, but instead with "disappointing" followed by "doesn't quite live up to its promise." Benefit occurs four times in the article. Twice it is compared to harms, once to risks, and once it occurs without the opposing term harm or risk. Breast cancer appears four times, and in each case the word death or mortality is in the same sentence. The other articles reporting the mammography harms research follow a similar pattern (see Table 2.1) where fear words like cancer and death, as well as benefit (of mammogram) are used more often than the words overdiagnosis, harm, and false positives. Those choices replay the cultural tendency to highlight fear of breast cancer and undercut information that shows screening in a negative light.

Vaccine Controversy Replays Oncogenic Assumptions

Like the breast cancer reporting, marketing, narratives, and screening recommendations, other conversations in public health, which involve multiple actors and narratives, focus action toward female bodies. When cancer enters the discourse, the attention to women intensifies reflecting integrated ideology about women's oncogenic nature. As such, the development and deployment of new vaccines to prevent human papilloma virus follow these well-worn paths, which require medical intervention for women and girls, overlooking men and boys. After Gardasil, an HPV vaccine, was approved by the FDA, Governor Perry of Texas issued a directive requiring parents to vaccinate girls, clearly focusing action on

Table 2.1 News media coverage of mammography overdiagnosis findings

TERMS	WA Post Bernstein	LA Times Morin	LA Times Kaplan	Denver Post Aschwanden (WaPo orig)	NY Times Kolata	NY Times Rabin
Mammography	5	10	4	7	19	7
Mammogram(s)	6	6	13	13	13	1
Breast cancer	4	7	12	7	10	3
Risk	4	1	0	3	0	1
Death	2	4	2	2	8	1
Dying	0	2	1	0	0	0
Cancer (s)	6	13	18	21	23	7
Benefits	4 (+ 1 title)	2	6	4	4	2
Save (s) (d)	3	0	2	7	1	1
Overdiagnos (is) (ed)	0	3	3	0	4	2
Harm(s) (ful)	3 (+ 1 title)	0	2	5	2	1
False Positive	1	0	0	1	1	1

female bodies, possibly against their will, and thus taking bodily autonomy from girls just learning to exercise it.

Attending to the claims in the press and marketing information surrounding the release of the Texas Gardasil mandate, as well as medical conversations imbedded therein, one sees that instead of a discussion about how to best prevent HPV related cancers in children, men, and women, the framing limits debate. Partially by using inaccurate language and addressing only female cancers, this discourse asks only whether, when, and how female body borders will be crossed by medical professionals. As Marie Thompson notes, these approaches to the vaccine "directly affect the health of both women and men, yet steadfastly focus on the female body" (120). Of course, all human bodies are permeable and penetrable, vulnerable to viruses. But perhaps because female bodies are routinely considered in terms of penetration, the defining point to be argued in the Gardasil conversation became about which types of medical penetration girls and women would endure and under what circumstances. Eventually, extensive critical treatment of both Perry's order and Gardasil marketing and policy emerged, including Wailoo et al.'s *Three Shots at Prevention*, Thompson's "Who's Guarding What?," and Globerson's "Protecting Women." For a feminist economic analysis see Melissa Haussman's *Reproductive Rights and the State*. Yet at the time, the choices presented in the debate include vaccination (chosen by state), and/or papanicolaou test (encouraged if not insisted upon by medical professionals), although discourse about the Gardasil mandate also veered to include sexual activity (hopefully chosen by the girl, but again constructed by parental notions of encouragement or discouragement). All of these real but very symbolic acts cross the borders of female bodies and reinforce public health interests in medical discipline of those bodies. Thus, the Gardasil example, like breast cancer pinkification, demonstrates how biomedical situations, even when procedures and drugs may have health benefits, adopt oncogenic narratives about female bodies to interpellate women into regimes of power and control.

In February 2007 Perry issued the executive order (Ex Or RP65) requiring all girls be immunized with Gardasil before entering the sixth grade in Texas schools. The "Rules" language "mandate the age appropriate vaccination of all female children for HPV prior to admission to the sixth grade" although verbiage "allow[s] *parents* to submit a request for a conscientious objection" (Ex Or RP65). In addition to the Texas Order, 41 states introduced legislation for the HPV vaccine, 25 of which suggested some sort of mandate, including Virginia's HB 2035/SB 1230, which compelled girls to obtain the HPV vaccine before beginning sixth grade (Jackson 2007). In August 2008, the US added Gardasil to the list of required vaccinations for (only) girls and women who immigrate to America; they cannot enter the country without it (Kimball).[9] Perry's order, while not the first to mandate the vaccine, provides a pertinent example of the rhetoric employed in a wide range of state and national health interventions surrounding Gardasil, and gendered health care interventions, public and private, through time. The constructed conversation remains limited to a yes or no decision, eliding more comprehensive health care conversations and constraining choices for female bodies. Even after the Texas mandate was overturned, the focus of state vaccination campaigns and Gardasil marketing remained on whether girls and women should accept medical treatments with possible bodily and social harms, while boys and men were not constructed as oncogenic nor asked to use their bodies to achieve the public health goal of reducing HPV rates.

In the Texas documents about Gardasil, key terms reappear providing an easy, albeit inaccurate way for political actors, medical professionals, and citizens to address the issue. These terms set the boundaries for argumentation about the issue, providing only one topic – the mandatory vaccination of girls – to be considered. For example, the second phrase in Governor Perry's executive order, states that "HPV is the most common sexually transmitted infection-causing cancer in females," thus focusing on how HPV affects female humans, and eliding HPV's effects on male bodies. He goes on to state that vaccination "protects women's health" (Perry), again leaving out how men's health might be protected.[10] While omission may not necessarily suggest the negation of harms to men, when coupled with the mandate only for girls, his official statement directs attention and action away from male bodies and toward presumed-oncogenic female bodies. Perry's declaration neatly alludes to some troubling enthymemes that plague Western discussion of female bodies: that they are other and weak, that they are always already sexualized, and that they should be medicalized and controlled. By connecting the term "sexually transmitted infection" to "females," and ignoring that this infection has negative effects on males as well – including cancers – the statement reminds the audience that female bodies are necessarily sexualized and reinforces the belief that their bodies are from the start, physically less efficient and more prone to cancer and thus in need of medical care. Rather than defining the disease and its effects, these tropes about women's bodies offer ready solutions that may not actually be solutions.

Beyond the cultural expectations of sexualized women, the rhetorical strategies used to discuss HPV locate risk in women's bodies. The opportune phrasing in Governor Perry's executive order further ignores the myriad ways that HPV viruses can also cause cancers in children of both genders and adult men, suggesting that female bodies rather than HPV viruses are the problem. As Wailoo et al. show "in their [girls] shadow stood young boys, whose own potential susceptibility to HPV- linked penile, anal, and oral cancers was . . . rendered invisible" (xiii). Boys and men contract and carry the virus, and they can develop as a result mouth, throat, anal, and penile cancers. The CDC reports "although the majority of infections cause no symptoms and are self-limited, persistent genital HPV infection can cause . . . anogenital cancers and genital warts in both men and women" ("Sexually" 2). Perry's statement intimates that the transition from HPV presence to cervical cancer is automatic and instantaneous, but HPV is not coterminous with cervical cancer. In an accompanying statement Perry opines that "Never before have we had an opportunity to prevent cancer with a simple vaccine." Of course, even the appearance of HPV 16 or 18 (virus types which relate to cervical cancer) does not mean that a woman will develop cancer, and not every cervical cancer is connected to HPV. The CDC points out that "the majority of women with high-risk HPV infection do not develop cancer" (Markowitz et al. 2). In Perry's statements, other HPV related disease like Laryngeal papillomas, oral cancers, penile and anal cancers, and hand, genital, and other skin warts, get effectively erased while public health fears and responsibilities get placed on women.[11] Perry's easy slide from STI to "causing cancer in females" erases other cancer attributable to HPV, conceals the actual probability of developing those multiple cancers, and confines the conversation to a dispute about whether or not to vaccinate women and girls. This definitional fixing precludes a larger conversation about impeding four HPV viruses and limits possible action to medical interventions on female bodies.

Beyond constructing a limited approach to HPV, the focus on cervical cancer belies the actual risk of that disease and leads to fears that promote women's compliance with medical directives. Actually, the CDC reported that, "Cervical cancer rates have decreased in the United States because of widespread use of Papanicolaou testing, . . . and that during 2007, . . . approximately 3,700 women will die from cervical cancer" (Markowitz et al. 1). If barely 3700 women per year die from cervical cancers in the US, when contrasted with the 696,947 deaths from heart disease in 2002, the need to vaccinate girls surely did not come from an epidemic of cervical cancer deaths. Yet, instead of a conversation about embodied health costs, as well as financial and cultural ones, the conversation ends at the fear of cervical cancer. Reminding girls and women of the dangers of cervical cancer encourages them to be fearful of disease that is specific to their reproductive organs, and allows boys and men to remain free of such fears. This discourse never approaches other ways of addressing HPV that do not involve singling out women as public health gatekeepers.

In the rhetorical conflation of HPV and cervical cancer, the burden of disease[12] ostensibly falls upon women, because most men cannot develop cancer of the cervix. This gendered expectation gets reflected in the clinical trials for Gardasil, which were correspondingly gendered. In the trials, men were tested for safety and immunogenicity but not efficacy (Villa et al.; Markowitz et al.). For clinical trials immunogenicity means that subjects have a capacity to create an immune response; for Gardasil that response would be to the four HPV viruses for which it was developed. The Committee on Immunization Practices reports that:

> Data on immunogenicity are available from Phase II (109) and Phase III double-blind, randomized, placebo-controlled trials conducted among females aged 16–26 years and immunogenicity studies conducted among males and females aged 9–15 years (113). In all studies conducted to date, >99% of study participants had an antibody response to all four HPV types in the vaccine 1 month after completing the 3-dose series (109,113). High seropositivity rates were observed after vaccination regardless of sex, ethnicity, country of origin, smoking status, or body mass index.
>
> (Markowitz et al. 15)

The immunogenicity phase trial results suggest that seropositivity rates are high in both males and females after vaccination, indicating success for both sexes. If the vaccine had been created to prevent cervical cancer rather than the virus, the procedure to test efficacy in women only may have made sense. Testing for efficacy involves conducting a study which will indicate whether a drug impacts a disease or condition, as opposed to effects on the isolated variable through which the drug functions. However, researchers **choose** the terms and markers for efficacy, when they design the study. In the American Gardasil trials, the disease, which represented efficacy was cervical intraepithelial dysplasia (CIN), an HPV disease that the majority of men cannot, by definition, contract. But as the vaccine, in point of fact, protects against four types of HPV and only two of them are related to cervical cancer, the choice to study CIN and only people with cervixes, predominantly women, in the efficacy phase was less than straightforward. According to Cosette Wheeler, researcher on some HPV vaccine clinical trials, the initial choice to test young women came from a ready supply of women attending for pap smears.[13] She also mentions that testing men for HPV involves taking swabs of mucosal areas, and scraping the cutaneous areas (penile shaft) with a swab (or low-grit sandpaper), something she maintains "they did not like" (Wheeler). There was no mention of whether the women enjoyed their tests.

While Dr. Wheeler's remark was casual, it reflects another cultural truism. Men do not like medical treatment or attention to their genitals, and their routine medical exams (when they happen) do not include extensive and invasive tests in the genital area, although they can sometimes include a hernia check or cursory exam. Women, on the other hand, are expected to treat their reproductive and sexual organs beginning in the teen years, regardless of discomfort or embarrassment. Foucault explained that "the hysterization of women . . . involved a thorough medicalization of their bodies and their sex . . . carried out in the name of the responsibility they owed to the health of their children . . . and the safe guarding of society" (146–147). If they wish to obtain oral contraceptives or other birth control, women may not be able to evade the pelvic exam and papanicolaou test. Leslie Reagan explains that "men are not subjected to these kinds of thorough physicals until a later age" (Reagan 1783).[14] In other words, teen boys and men expect bodily autonomy and the right to make medical decisions for their own comfort rather than the public health good, while women are trained to relinquish bodily autonomy and endure personal discomfort under pressure from health care practitioners and the larger culture. This expectation reinforces a culturally accepted construct that women's bodies and sexual organs must be medically ministered in order to create the next generation. Marie Thompson maintains that "men's sexuality is rarely linked to their role as potential fathers, while women continue to be held and seen as largely responsible for their and their partners' education in matters of reproductive health" (121). Examples like the Gardasil campaign display how health care practices and the conversations surrounding cancer prevention can become cultural contact points to jeopardize women's bodily autonomy.

The Gardasil vaccine movement, which planned to vaccinate only female adults and preteen girls rather than all children of a certain age, fits elegantly into existing over-medicalization of girls and women in Western culture. Lois Verbrugge's article "Gender & Health" presents data that shows males aged 15–44 visited the doctor 1667 times per 1000 population in 1979 in contrast to the 3068 times per 1000 population for females in the same range (160). Her research suggests that women are trained to accept invasive medical observations and penetrations beginning in their teen years.[15] Teenage boys, on the other hand, are attenuating regular pediatrician visits as "male adolescents frequently become disconnected from health care" (Marcell et al. 967). Discrepancies between the genders' health care use decreases with age, but in young people, women and girls are far more likely to attend doctor visits and comply with health directives. Leslie Reagan explains how "women had long been educated to go in for examinations and, because of childbearing, had endured more observation and touching of their genitals by doctors. Men did not have comparable medical experiences" (1783). The Gardasil mandate(s) goes further, encouraging preteen girls to believe that they have no say in whether medical authorities will touch their bodies, *against their will* or not. Lack of consent is surely not a healthy lesson for developing young people to internalize, and as Catriona Mackenzie foregrounds in her work, "respect for a person's body is an integral part of respect for the person" (420–421). She goes on to claim "an intimate connection between our bodies and our selfhood is of course well known to oppressors" (421). This link between control over one's own body and freedom from oppression becomes crucial for young women, whose control over their bodies has historically been denied by institutions, including medicine.

Such extended and invasive contact with the health industry teaches young women and the culture around them that female bodies are penetrable by specula, spatulas, brushes, and needles, regardless of comfort or consent. After Governor Perry's order was rescinded, the American approach to Gardasil continued for some time to encourage women and teen and preteen girls, but not men and boys to undergo vaccination. As the pressure continues, girls and women learn that medical penetrations are not really a matter of their own choice. In her article "Gracious Submission" Susan Shaw explains that "to deny women the right to make their own decisions at this most intimate level of the self [body] is to deny them selfhood, subjectivity, and agency" (55). Her research suggests that early lessons to cede bodily control to health care providers can reinforce other cultural cues about sovereignty for women's bodies. At a time when boys and girls are learning to develop independence and exercise health judgment, health directives like the Gardasil campaign only exaggerate the differences between what is expected of boys and girls, men and women. While some might argue that additional medical attention is an intrinsic good, the fact that public health campaigns reinforce discrepancies in medical interventions along gender lines should prompt thoughtful dialogue about the effect of such directives on both women and men.

Unfortunately, health care directives often suggest that women's bodies should provide a benefit for the public health, placing women in the position of health gatekeepers, even when evidence undercuts that direction. For HPV protection, *The Vaccine Book*, written before Gardasil had been fully tested, suggests that any future HPV vaccination "must include males and females in order to reduce the virus load within the population" (Bloom 317), a concept informally described as herd immunity. Since the Texas case, questions about male disease and male vaccination appeared, but herd immunity was absent from early Gardasil discourse. Anne Kimball also reflects on:

> The questionable wisdom of the public health policy being used with respect to the HPV vaccine. Merck . . . has not completed testing or sought approval for use in young males – as men are also susceptible to certain forms of HPV and are known carriers of HPV strains that can cause cervical cancer, there is weak public health justification for not seeking approval for the vaccine for males and making a similar recommendation that young males receive the vaccine.
>
> (Kimball)

Kimball's observations critique the way that Gardasil policies reinforce medicalization of women's bodies, but her focus solely on cervical cancer replays social discourse about cancerous female organs.

Discourse about women's and girl's bodies reinforce unhealthy messages about bodily and social self-government, messages that can contribute to other cultural ills. If medical authorities, instead of women and girls themselves, make decisions about where and when female bodies may be penetrated, surely that suggests that other agents can decide for women and girls if and when their bodies are accessible. Similarly, arguments that place responsibility for public health on women and girls, undercut the ability for those individuals to make their own decisions about their bodies. Instead, female bodies become de facto public (health) property. These health care regimes of power entail additional interpellations for women; doctor visits also cost girls and women time and money, while integrating them into data collection and reporting systems with potential for abuse. This suggests that while Gardasil and similar vaccines which protect against HPV may be useful medicines, the gendered practices by which they were initially positioned and marketed both reflect and contribute to troubling attitudes in the healthcare system and in our culture, attitudes that label women's bodies oncogenic and disallow women from making health care choices for themselves, and exempt boys and men from responsibility for the public health. Yet the perceived and real porousness of sexed and gendered bodies can be better addressed with an attention to the porousness of medical definitions and solutions and with a more open conversation about both.

Changing Oncogenic Assumptions

In the intervening years since the Texas Gardasil mandate, policies and attitudes about vaccinating boys and men for HPV have shifted somewhat, moving away from locating risk for HPV in "marginalized bodies" toward "a shared specificity and vulnerability" (Scott 89). Current CDC recommendations suggest "All kids who are 11 or 12 years old should get two shots of HPV vaccine" and explains HPV's effects on cancers in the cervix, vagina, vulva, penis, anus, back of the throat "including the base of the tongue and tonsils (oropharynx)" (CDC "HPV"). In addition to changes in Gardasil promotion, mammography recommendations have altered somewhat to reflect research that uncovered overdiagnosis of breast cancer. The CDC now follows the USPSTF guidelines suggesting that women begin regular mammography at 50 rather than 40 years (CDC "What Is"), although the Mayo clinic maintains an earlier date, "Mayo Clinic supports screening beginning at age 40" (Mammogram). Mayo's decision reflects clinical, social, and economic factors that cannot be easily untangled, but maintains a fear-producing rhetorical choice with material consequences to women's embodied experience. Transferring biomedical indications away from women represents a positive trend, while unable to erase the tendency of early cancer care directives to array toward female bodies as Moscucci displays how "women's cancers have played an outstanding role in positioning cancer in the public domain" (1). Yet, shifting the focus away from women's monstrous and oncogenic bodies in some parts of the culturescape builds away from assumptions that undergirded earlier choices.

In examining the medical documents and cultural artifacts that form an American conversation about cancer, a recurring persuasive message appears suggesting female bodies naturally, passively, and almost inevitably develop cancer, especially in the breast and cervix, organs related to reproductive capacities. These messages reflect a willingness to create fear of specific cancers in women and a subsequent emphasis on what Foucault might label disciplinary screening and intervention upon the bodies of women and girls, a tendency we will see recreated in early Kenyan attention to cancer. Julie Livingston notes current differences in cancer realities from the two continents suggesting that unlike cancer care in Botswana "in North America the rise of screening technologies and mass screening efforts mean that such precancers and early cancers are regularly discovered in women's bodies, and . . . have important effects. They propel women into surgery and more intensified forms of surveillance" (53). Despite existing distinctions in cancer care and beliefs, the Western culturescape Livingston describes, infused with acceptance of the trope of oncogenic women, provides a starting point for investigation of transmission of these biomedical messages, attitudes, and practices to developing countries like Kenya through globalizing efforts exporting cancer technologies and methods.

Notes

1. Current USPSTF materials reinforce men's agency and decision-making ability "For men aged 55 to 69 years, the decision to undergo periodic prostate-specific antigen (PSA) – based screening for prostate cancer should be an individual one." Language about individual choice reigns in prostate cancer screening conversations.
2. See www.goodreads.com/shelf/show/breast-cancer for a list of popular breast cancer books.
3. See Kicki Klaeson, Sandell, and Bertero, "Sexuality in the Context of Prostate Cancer Narratives" Qual Health Res 2012 22:1184 for use of the term "prostate narratives" in a different context.
4. See Barron Lerner *The Breast Cancer Wars: Hope, Fear, and the Pursuit of a Cure in Twentieth-Century America.* For full treatment of Komen and pinkification, see King, Samantha. *Pink Ribbons: Breast Cancer and the Politics of Philanthropy.* See also Pezzullo, Phaedro; and Kopelson, Karen. "Risky Appeals"
5. Breast cancer occurs in men, albeit infrequently.
6. Policy around screening is becoming increasingly contested as cost/benefit analyses in the health field become increasingly fine-tuned. See, for example, Louise B. Russell, *Educated Guesses.*
7. Gilbert Welch et al. suggest "only 30 of the 162 additional small tumors per 100,000 women that were diagnosed were expected to progress to become large, which implied that the remaining 132 cases of cancer per 100,000 women were overdiagnosed" (1438).
8. See ongoing debate about and reticence to administer PSA tests. For example, Fenton et al. report, "PSA screening may reduce prostate cancer mortality risk but is associated with false-positive results, biopsy complications, and overdiagnosis. Compared with conservative approaches, active treatments for screen-detected prostate cancer have unclear effects on long-term survival but are associated with sexual and urinary difficulties" (1929). Research here foregrounds iatrogenic outcomes for male bodies rather than benefits and unlike the mammogram debate, recommendations at Mayo clinic and elsewhere reflect the actual research explaining "There is a lot of conflicting advice about PSA testing. To decide whether to have a PSA test, discuss the issue with your doctor, considering your risk factors and weighing your *personal preferences*" (Mayo,

PSA my emphasis). Unlike with mammography screening, Mayo places agency in individual men. See also Mara in Frost and Eble.
9. Kimball explains that "the vaccine is the only mandated vaccine for green-card applicants that is not meant to fight infectious diseases that are transmitted by a respiratory route" (1). This vaccine mandate surely places a larger burden on girls and women who wish to immigrate to the US, making an already precarious situation for some women even more difficult.
10. Perry himself conflates the preteen girls affected by the executive order with "women," creating a singular category based on gender and eschewing questions of difference between girls and women.
11. According to Sinal and Woods, "Laryngeal papillomas, the primary form of JO-RRP, are the most common tumor of the larynx in childhood worldwide. Prevalence of JO-RRP is approximately 1.7 to 2.6 per 100,000 children in the United States. Boys and girls are represented nearly equally among children with JO-RRP" (2005).
12. Burden of disease refers to the "total significance of disease" (WHO), including disability and the number of years by which lives are shortened by disease either globally or for specific populations.
13. Personal phone interview March 9, 2008.
14. Even the body border crossing Digital Rectal Exam (DRE), which older men endure to test for prostate cancer has been supplemented and in some cases replaced with a less invasive blood test for Prostate-Specific Antigen (PSA). Some men simply refuse to accept such bodily incursions, and the medical field accommodates them, finding less invasive ways to address men's health. To date there has been no blood test developed to replace papanicolaou tests, and Cosette Wheeler expressed doubt there would be.
15. The data reporting routine doctor visits, of course, includes private medical care, which is marketed more heavily toward women, but the cultural effects of medicalization become starker when public health choices and mandates reflect the tendency to treat women's bodies rather than men's.

Works Cited

Appadurai, Arjun. *Modernity at Large: Cultural Dimensions of Globalization*. U of Minnesota P, 1996.
Aristotle. *Generation of Animals*. Translated by A.L Peck. Harvard UP, 1942.
Aschwanden, Christie. "Questioning Mammograms: Is the Test Worth Having?" *Denver Post,* 19 Mar. 2014.
Bernstein, Lenny. "Despite Strong Benefits, Mammograms May Have Greater Harms Than Previously Realized, Study Says." *The Washington Post,* Health & Science, 1 Apr. 2014.
Biller-Andorno, Nikola, and Peter Jüni. "Abolishing Mammography Screening Programs? A View from the Swiss Medical Board." *The New England Journal of Medicine*, vol. 370, no. 21, 2014, pp. 1965–67.
Bloom, Barry R., and Paul-Henri Lambert. *The Vaccine Book*. Elsevier Science, 2003.
Cancer Facts and Figures 2016. "American Cancer Society," www.cancer.org/content/dam/cancer-org/research/cancer-facts-and-statistics/annual-cancer-facts-and-figures/2016/cancer-facts-and-figures-2016.pdf

Center for Disease Control (CDC). "HPV Vaccines: Vaccinating Your Preteen or Teen," www.cdc.gov/hpv/parents/vaccine.html
———. "Sexually Transmitted Diseases Treatment Guidelines 2006," www.cdc.gov/STD/treatment/2006/specialpops.htm. Accessed 23 June 2007.
———. "What is Breast Cancer Screening?" www.cdc.gov/cancer/breast/basic_info/screening.htm. Accessed Sept. 2018.
Chopra, Sonia. "Review of Good Harbor, Curled up with a Good Book," 2002, www.curledup.com/gdharbor.htm
Comeau, Tammy Duerden. "Gender Ideology and Disease Theory: Classifying Cancer in Nineteenth Century Britain." *Journal of Historical Sociology*, vol. 20, nos. 1–2, 2007, pp. 158–81.
Courtenay, Will H. "Constructions of Masculinity and Their Influence on Men's Well-being: A Theory of Gender and Health." *Social Science & Medicine*, vol. 50, no. 10, 2000, pp. 1385–401.
Diamant, Anita. *Good Harbor*. Scribner, 2002.
Douda, Dennis. "Breast Cancer Screening Guidelines Revised." Mayo Clinic News Network, Oct. 2015, https://newsnetwork.mayoclinic.org/discussion/breast-cancer-screening-guidelines-revised/
Fenton, Joshua J. et al. "Prostate-Specific Antigen – Based Screening for Prostate Cancer: Evidence Report and Systematic Review for the US Preventive Services Task Force." *JAMA*, vol. 319, no. 18, 2018, pp. 1914–31.
Fosket, Jennifer Ruth. "Breast Cancer Risk as Disease: Biomedicalizing Risk." *Biomedicalization: Technoscience, Health, and Illness in the U.S.*, edited by Adele Clarke et al., Duke UP, 2010, pp. 331–52.
Foucault, Michel. *The History of Sexuality*. 1st American ed. New York: Pantheon, 1978.
Globerson, Micah. "Protecting Women: A Feminist Legal Analysis of The HPV Vaccine, Gardasil." *Texas Journal of Women and the Law*, vol. 17, no. 1, 2007, pp. 67–107.
Haussman, Melissa et al. *Reproductive Rights and the State Getting the Birth Control, RU-486, Morning-after Pills and the Gardasil Vaccine to the U.S. Market*. Praeger, 2013.
Holloway, Karla. *Private Bodies, Public Texts: Race, Gender, and a Cultural Bioethics*. Duke UP, 2011.
Horner, Gail. 2004. "Genital Warts in Children: Sexual Abuse or Not?" *Journal of Pediatric Health Care*, vol. 18, no. 4, 2004, pp. 165–70.
Jackson, Lauren. "HPV Vaccine and State Mandates." *Wisconsin Briefs from the Legislative Reference Bureau*, Brief 07–7. LRB–07–WB–7, Sept. 2004, www.legis.state.wi.us/lrb.
Kaplan, Karen. "Mammograms Save Lives, But They're Also Overrated, New Study Says." *LA Times*, Science, 2 Apr. 2014.
Kimball, Anne S. "HPV Vaccine Debate Meets the International Stage." *Health Law Perspectives*, Health Law & Policy Institute, U of Houston, Oct. 2008, www.law.uh.edu/healthlaw/perspectives/homepage.asp.
King, Samantha. *Pink Ribbons: Breast Cancer and the Politics of Philanthropy*. U of Minnesota P, 2006.

Kolata, Gina. "Vast Study Cast Doubts on Value of Mammograms." *New York Times*, Health, 12 Feb. 2014.

Kopelson, Karen. "Risky Appeals: Recruiting to the Environmental Breast Cancer Movement in the Age of 'Pink Fatigue.'" *Rhetoric Society Quarterly*, vol. 43, no. 2, 2013, pp. 107–33.

Latour, Bruno. *Reassembling the Social an Introduction to Actor-Network-Theory*. Oxford UP, 2005.

Lerner, Barron H. *The Breast Cancer Wars: Hope, Fear, and the Pursuit of a Cure in Twentieth-Century America*. Oxford UP, 2001.

Livingston, Julie. *Improvising Medicine: An African Oncology Ward in an Emerging Cancer Epidemic*. Duke UP, 2012.

Mackenzie, Catriona. "On Bodily Autonomy." *Handbook of Phenomenology and Medicine*, edited by S. Kay Toombs. Springer, 2001, pp. 417–40.

"Mammograms." Fact Sheet. National Cancer Institute, www.cancer.gov/types/breast/mammograms-fact-sheet

Mara, Miriam. "Bras, Bros, and Colons: How Even the Mayo Clinic Gets it Wrong Gendering Cancer." *Interrogating Gendered Pathologies*, Eds Michele Eble and Erin Frost, Utah State UP, forthcoming 2020.

Marcell, Arik V. et al. "Masculine Beliefs, Parental Communication, and Adolescents' Health Care Use." *Pediatrics*, vol. 119, no. 4, Apr. 2007, pp. 966–75.

Marcoux, Danielle et al. "Pediatric Anogenital Warts: A 7-Year Review of Children Referred to a Tertiary-Care Hospital in Montreal, Canada." *Pediatric Dermatology*, vol. 23, no. 3, 2006, pp. 199–207.

Markowitz, Lauri E. et al. "Quadrivalent Human Papillomavirus Vaccine: Recommendations of the Advisory Committee on Immunization Practices (ACIP)." CDC, 56 (RR02) 1–24, 23 Mar. 2007, www.cdc.gov/mmwr/preview/mmwrhtml/rr5602a1.htm

"Mayo Clinic Tests and Procedures: Mammogram Guidelines," www.mayoclinic.org/tests-procedures/mammogram/expert-answers/mammogram-guidelines/faq-20057759

"Mayo Clinic Tests and Procedures: PSA Test," www.mayoclinic.org/tests- procedures/psa-test/about/pac-20384731

Miller, Anthony B. et al. "Twenty Five Year Follow-up for Breast Cancer Incidence and Mortality of the Canadian National Breast Screening Study: Randomised Screening Trial." *British Medical Journal*, vol. 348, no. 9, 11 Feb. 2014, p. 366.

Morin, Monte. "Mammogram Screenings Don't Reduce Cancer Death Rates, Study Finds." *LA Times*. Science, 11 Feb. 2014.

Mosca, Lori Marie et al. "Tracking Women's Awareness of Heart Disease: An American Heart Association National Study." *Circulation: Journal of the American Heart Association*, vol. 109, no. 5, 2004, pp. 573–79.

Moscucci, Ornella. *Gender and Cancer in England, 1860–1948*. Palgrave, 2016.

National Postal Museum. "Arago: People: Postage & the Post," https://arago.si.edu

Pace, Lydia E., and Nancy L. Keating. "A Systematic Assessment of Benefits and Risks to Guide Breast Cancer Screening Decisions." *JAMA*, vol. 311, no. 13, 2014, pp. 1327–35.

Perry, Rick. Executive Order RP65 "Relating to the Immunization of Young Women from the Cancer-causing Human Papillomavirus." Austin, TX, 2 Feb. 2007.

———. "Statement of Gov. Rick Perry on HPV Vaccine Executive Order." Austin, 5 Feb. 2007.
Pezzullo, Phaedra C. "Resisting 'National Breast Cancer Awareness Month': The Rhetoric of Counterpublics and Their Cultural Performances." *Quarterly Journal of Speech*, vol. 89, no. 4, 2003, pp. 345–65.
Rabin, Roni Caryn. "For Women, a More Complicated Choice on Mammograms." *New York Times*, Health, 11 Feb. 2014.
Reagan, Leslie J. "Engendering the Dread Disease: Women, Men and Cancer." *American Journal of Public Health*, vol. 87, no. 11, 1997, pp. 1779–86.
Russell, Louise B., and Milbank Memorial Fund. *Educated Guesses: Making Policy About Medical Screening Tests*. U of California P, 1994.
Scott, J. Blake. *Risky Rhetoric: Aids and the Cultural Practices of HIV Testing*. Southern Illinois UP, 2003.
Segal, Judy Z. "Breast Cancer Narratives as Public Rhetoric: Genre Itself and the Maintenance of Ignorance." *Linguistics and the Human Sciences*, vol. 3, no. 1, 2008, pp. 3–23.
Selleck, Laurie. "Pretty in Pink: The Susan G. Koman Network and the Branding of the Breast Cancer Cause." *Nordic Journal of English Studies* (*NJES*), vol. 9, no. 3, 2010, pp. 119–38.
Shaw, Susan. "Gracious Submissions: Southern Baptist Fundamentalists and Women." *NWSA Journal*, vol. 20, no. 1, 2008, pp. 51–77.
Sinal, Sara H. and Charles R. Woods. "Human Papillomavirus Infections of the Genital and Respiratory Tracts in Young Children." *Seminars in Pediatric Infectious Diseases*, vol. 16, no. 4, 2005, pp. 306–16.
Thompson, Marie. "Who's Guarding What? A Poststructural Feminist Analysis of Gardasil Discourses." *Health Communication*, vol. 25, no. 2, 2010, pp. 119–30.
United States Postal Service (USPS). "Semipostal Stamp Program," https://about.usps.com/corporate-social-responsibility/semipostals.htm
U.S. Cancer Statistics Working Group. *United States Cancer Statistics: 2004 Incidence and Mortality*. Centers for Disease Control and Prevention, 2004.
U.S. Preventative Services Task Force. "Final Recommendation Statement *Prostate Cancer: Screening*," www.uspreventiveservicestaskforce.org/Page/Document/Recommendation StatementFinal/prostate-cancer-screening1
———. "USPSTF Still Recommends Mammography for Women 50–74," www.aafp.org/news/health-of-the-public/20150424mammograms.html
"Vaccination Requirements for IV Applicants." U.S. Department of State, http://travel.state.gov/visa/immigrants/info/info_1331.html
Verbrugge, Lois M. "Gender & Health: An Update on Hypotheses and Evidence." *Journal of Health and Social Behavior*, vol. 26, no. 3, 1985, pp. 156–82.
Villa, L.L. et al. "Prophylactic Quadrivalent Human Papillomavirus (Types 6, 11, 16, and 18) L1 Virus-like Particle Vaccine in Young Women: A Randomised Double- blind Placebo-controlled Multicentre Phase II Efficacy Trial." *Lancet, Oncology*, vol. 6, 2005, pp. 271–78.
Wailoo, Keith et al., editors. *Three Shots at Prevention: The HPV Vaccine and the Politics' of Medicine's Simple Solutions*. The Johns Hopkins UP, 2010.

Welch, H. Gilbert, et al. "Breast-Cancer Tumor Size, Overdiagnosis, and Mammography Screening Effectiveness." *The New England Journal of Medicine*, vol. 375, no. 15, 2016, pp. 1438–47.

Wheeler, Cosette. Phone Interview in discussion with the author, 9 Mar. 2008.

World Health Organization. "Health Systems: Concepts, Design & Performance," www.emro.who.int/mei/mep/Healthsystemsglossary.htm

Yadlon, Susan. "Skinny Women and Good Mothers: The Rhetoric of Risk, Control, and Culpability in the Production of Knowledge about Breast Cancer." *Feminist Studies*, vol. 23, no. 3, 1997, pp. 645–77.

3 Tracing Kenya's Culturescape

Cancer as Gendered Weakness in *Place of Destiny*

As the leading economy in Eastern Africa until Ethiopia gained that status in 2017, Kenya is still poised between postcolonial tension and global capitalism. Gaining independence from England in 1963, Kenya rapidly achieved economic strength and a tenuous political equilibrium. Despite violent demonstrations after the 2007 elections when Mwai Kibaki became president in a power-sharing deal, Kenya displays fewer of the ethnic or tribal conflicts of the larger region. The reality of ethnic differences, human rights abuses, and election disparities did recur in the 2016 reelection of President Uhuru Kenyatta, creating the necessity for a repeat election, but massive, country-wide violence was avoided. Current strains on Kenya include tensions with Somalia, recurrent corruption incidents, and economic pressure from hosting Somali, South Sudanese, and other refugees. Kenya still bears huge economic disparity partially caused by corruption in government and the legacy of colonialism, yet it represents an African success story. By Western standards "there is minimal [biomedical] infrastructure for cancer care in Kenya" (Strother et al. 26), but that is quickly changing. In Nairobi, the capital and the second largest city in Eastern Africa, three large hospitals, Nairobi Hospital, Aga Khan Hospital, and Kenyatta National Hospital, as well as Nairobi Women's Hospital, Karen Hospital, and a number of small private hospitals, which Americans might compare to urgent care clinics, proffer contemporary Western biomedicine; in smaller cities and rural areas – and, to a lesser degree, Nairobi as well – traditional healers and herbalists treat up to 80% of Kenya's population. Despite traditional healers providing the majority of health care, many political and social power structures favor biomedicine and eschew traditional healing, perhaps connected to postcolonial identity fissures. Efforts to build infrastructure and encourage (bio)medical *development* provide ready pathways for Western attitudes about health and gendered bodies. This liminal, conflicted, partially westernized space provides a fitting space to study how biomedicalization influences cancer understandings and cancer treatment in a developing country because biomedical cancer practices are slowly entering Kenya's larger culturescape, especially in the capital.

One way to investigate the culturescape comes through celebrated fiction, especially texts with cancer-focused narratives. Margaret Ogola is one of Kenya's best-known novelists. While Ngugi Wa Thiong'O gained more popularity in the United States, Ogola gained a following in Kenya and throughout Africa. Her first novel, *The River and the Source*, which documents the lives of four Kenyan women, won the 1995 Commonwealth Writers' Prize for Best First Book in Africa and subsequently became part of the standard curriculum in literature for Kenyan students. Like Wangari Maathai, who won the Nobel Prize for her work founding the Greenbelt Movement, Ogola was also an activist and used her medical degree and notoriety to care for AIDS orphans in Nairobi. Ogola was known both for her interest in women's empowerment and for her somewhat conservative ideas about how to achieve progress for women. Her novels always create strong female characters, but those characters usually must also engage in traditional roles of caretaking and reproduction. Her last novel, *Place of Destiny*, received mixed reviews because of its unsubtle religious message, still winning second place for the 2007 Jomo Kenyatta Prize for Literature. Gikandi and Mwangi suggest that *Destiny* "didactically explores themes of suffering, grief . . . and life after death" (131). Beyond those themes, the text provides a fictional account of cancer from the pen of someone with a medical background from the University of Nairobi, which at one time was affiliated with University of London. As such, this novel becomes an important culturescape artifact, where medical attitudes and cultural assumptions, partially transferred from Western origins through global flows, mesh. As Karla Holloway illuminates "although law and medicine are rigorously practical fields not much given to the imaginary, literature's stories can encourage our substantive notice and consideration of the ethics embedded within both disciplines" (10). An analysis of the gendered representations of cancer in *Destiny* illustrates how uncomplicated ideas about women and women's bodies are translated into attitudes about cancer and its treatment.

The text follows two families dealing with illness, focusing on the final months of Amore Lore and Igana Magu, both of whom have developed cancer. Lore's husband Mrema and her adult children initially struggle to deal with her diagnosis because her strength has maintained the relationships up to this point. Lore's double, Igana Magu also develops cancer, but he initially has no family relationships to maintain, since he is divorced and estranged from his difficult parents. Magu discovers his nephew, Dr. Igana Mago, when he first visits the hospice center where late stage cancer patients receive palliative care. Mago, son of the sister who ran away at the novel's opening, becomes the focal point for the family's connections.

Eventually, Dr. Mago, who is also Lore's hospice physician, marries her daughter Imani, and both extended families heal as a result of the bonding between the two groups and the subsequent reconciliations within each family.

A Failed Feminist Text?

Ostensibly, Ogola creates a feminist text that identifies unfair attitudes about gender in contemporary Kenya. As Ogola scholar Tom Odhiambo notes, her first novel "rightfully can be described as a landmark in Kenya's postcolonial literary history, especially because of its unapologetic privileging of women and womanhood" (236). Nici Nelson too suggests that Kenyan "women novelists [like Ogola] are renegotiating the representations of men and women in their writing" (167). Alina Rinkanya posits Ogola's second novel *I Swear by Apollo* as an attempt to "draw an ideal picture of her country... 'Kenya as it should be', the ideal state created by an ideal leader, the first female President" (150), a markedly feminist text, and Felicia Yieke calls it "gender sensitive" (343). *Place of Destiny*, like the earlier novels, creates strong female characters and performs analysis of gender oppression in Kenya. The novel's representation of the work lives of women and men displays awareness about distribution of effort versus distribution of wealth. In her study of theater in Ghana, Catherine Cole suggests that "while gender posits an inclusive, relational analysis that intersects with, but is not determined by, physical sex, those who are physically sexed as female in Africa still have far less access than men do to material resources and political power. That discrepancy must not slip from view" (270–271). Cole's analysis shows growth in the theater in West Africa shows growth in representation of women, moving away from misogynist tropes, which she connects to actual changes in women's work both in the theater and in other public spaces, such as education and politics. Cole maintains that gender remains a theoretically and practically rich area of study in Africa. Her study uses literature – plays – and historical information about women entering the theater as actors and writers to interrogate the premise that Africa might be post-gender or at least may not have gender problems that correlate with gender issues in the West. Ogola's last novel may invite similar post-gender readings, as it attends to changing opportunities for women in Kenya, but in segments, *Place of Destiny* still betrays gender as a limiting factor for women. In fact, Ogola's opening treatment of a young mother, who turns to prostitution as a means to care for her son contains seeds of criticism about male domination in sexual matters within Kenya.

Additionally, the text presents women who take on positions of power and succeed in many fields, often in direct competition with men. The protagonist, Amor Lore, who is one successful woman, unpacks the unfair gender situation describing her brothers' family workload as nothing "heavier than holding a stick and following our small herd of scrawny zebus, fat-tailed sheep and half-wild goats to the grazing fields where they would laze their weekends away playing games with others also fortunate enough to be born with the right kind of reproductive equipment" (Ogola 19). Lore's sarcastic tone and withering evaluation of male work ethic indicate that this female character, at least, understands feminist ideals and agrees that gender equality would improve Kenyan society. If the powerful women characters and this individual character's gender critiques represent a feminist outlook, then the text could be named feminist. Lore and her daughters all represent strong, and in some cases actually powerful, characters. Yet this novel contains non-feminist and essentialist attitudes about female bodies and gendered illness that come from Western medicine and travel through globalized health care; those negative biases about women's bodies seep into the otherwise feminist narrative.

One essentialist attitude, which limits women's available life choices and thus may be anti-feminist, is the emphasis on reproduction as the most important part of female experience. While the narrative admits to the burden reproduction can place on women, it remains a pro-natalist text. Similar importance gets placed on women's reproductive abilities in the United States "not simply in the area of health care but in more general cultural representation, where women have been either invisible as a separate category or traditionally positioned as reproducers, regardless of any individual intention or ability to exercise that capacity" (Shildrik 22). Openly pro-natal environments like Kenya also focus on reproduction, and Ogola's work is no different. The novel begins with a pregnant young girl "only sixteen, perhaps seventeen, but she was heavy with child and with deep unhappiness" (Ogola 9), reminding readers from the outset that reproduction is part of women's lives and that it affects their bodies as well as their fates. This pregnant young woman appears in the very first sentence, and the syntax places her pregnancy in tandem with and parallel to her sadness. The idea that childbearing connects to women's unhappiness does not recur in the text, but this admission sets the tone for the gendered narrative that follows.

As the idea that bearing children might be a struggle worth evaluating more carefully disappears after this chapter, it seems incongruous that the idea has the prominent placement of being the first sentence of the text. For Amor Lore, childbearing and parenting represent joyful experiences in life, which seems incompatible with the novel's first sentence. Even the successful life of the grown child born of the young prostitute from the tragic first chapter undercuts the novel's opening. The son she bears, Igano Mago, becomes a hero in the text, serving as hospice doctor to Ms. Lore and eventually marrying her daughter. The positive outcomes proffered to the offspring of the oppressed young girl could add nuance to her extremely negative experience. Instead the narrative choices to make her son so successful and integral to the narrative and to quickly remove this poor woman from the text completely, killing her off in the first chapter, quash any feminist discussion about how reproduction burdens women. The sad young woman who disappears begets a son, who thinks to himself, "And like any normal person, I'd love to have children" (108). The suffering of his mother becomes inconsequential because he, the product of her miserable pregnancy and catalyst for her turn to prostitution, has fared well. Despite the text opening with such a negative image of motherhood, for Mago, and indeed for most characters in the text, desire for children represents the norm, especially for professional people. There are no women in the text who focus on their careers to the extent that they forego childbearing and raising children, despite the reality that some career-driven women do so, and the mothers in the text have no apparent trouble with balancing children with work.

Even the complaints about men's aversion to work – which are so close to being a feminist critique – get undercut by the text's representation of the primary male characters. Lore's husband, Mwaghera Mrema, shows a continued passion for historical research, and Mago is exceptionally dedicated to his patients. Mago "work[s] in this hospice by choice, to try and ameliorate a little, the suffering of the dying" (69). The characters and the narrator remark upon his dedication on numerous occasions. Mrema, too, maintains a passion for his work in historical scholarship, suggesting that not all Kenyan men partake of the laziness ascribed to Lore's brothers. In these ways, the text destabilizes much of the early chapters' complaints about gender relations in Kenya, and diminish the feminist critique. The effect of more positive than negative male characters allows the narrative to veer away from any real criticism of gender imbalances in Kenyan culture.

These men Mago and Mrema salvage male character, just as later events recover parenthood, making it seem appealing and necessary. An important facet of Lore's character is motherhood. We learn very early that she has "a son and three daughters all of whom [she's] inordinately proud" (17) somewhat before she announces that she has "a Master's degree in Business Administration" (17). These details about her intellectual and financial success develop more, but then they recede from the narrative. The early section hints at her power in the business sector when Lore explains, "I like my financial independence. There is an incredible sense of power and freedom in being able to direct money" (33), yet the most important *business* decision readers see is placing a certain two people together on a project. Putting these two together might very well suit Lore in a business sense, but she aims, more importantly according to the text, to matchmake. As the text winds down after Lore's death, we find that the two colleagues have in fact become a couple. More important to the text than her success in business or in matchmaking, Lore has four children who become characters of import as the text progresses. When she considers the positive reasons for a slower death, her children's well-being becomes the focus: "Since I am their mother and am the one who is dying, I decide that the gentlest thing would be for me to tell them. It is for this reason that I have been spared a sudden death. It is for this reason that I am not comatose and hooked up to all kinds of machines" (65). Lore's assistant describes her as inscrutable and tough, but this section addressing the children concerns her "gentlest" way of proceeding. While much of the beautiful description in this novel centers around Lore's relationship with her husband, she ascribes the extended period of planning as extra time to tell her children about the disease. The adjective "gentle" does not get applied often in this text, but in the context of communication with her children, Lore is suddenly concerned with gentleness. This attention not just to a husband and counterpart but to her offspring mark the importance of the parenting role to the dying woman in this text.

Despite her superlative language about her husband, when she claims that "as always [her] heart skips a beat at the sight of him" (27), Lore focuses on the children just as much as on her husband. In fact, while the novel insists on Lore's success as a business person – "I have, over time, chanced on a niche in the market place of human affairs for which I have an unusual talent and I have made money in the process" (33) – her motherhood becomes more important as the text progresses. When it begins, she is in her office contemplating business, but her children quickly move into the foreground. That she self-identifies as "a woman of action" (28) does interrupt tired stereotypes of passive women, but her action during the course of the text mostly involves taking care of her family, planning for her death, and enduring illness. Lore acts by gathering her husband and children to her and comforting them even as she herself is the one dying.

More important than the reproductive and nurturing roles enforced for women characters, is the portrayal of female bodies as inherently weak and damaged, essentially oncogenic. Especially in terms of the gendered body, *Place of Destiny* creates a hierarchy where men are stronger, self-determined, and more connected to their reasoning, whereas women are weak, passive, and corporeal. In her article about African fiction that undercut problematic tropes about black women and infection, Giuliana Lund explains how "the pathological qualities of the African environment were thus embodied for Europeans in the African woman" (163). The representation of illness through African female bodies that Lund describes provides a troubling context for understanding Ogola's novel. These attitudes spring partially from long-held biases in medicine. As Marianne Van Den Wijngaard elucidates in her study *Reinventing the Sexes: The Biomedical Construction of Femininity and Masculinity*, "a danger inherent in almost all dualistic thought (and certainly in the duality of masculinity and femininity) is that one half of the duality is assigned a superior significance" (109). She goes on to provide specific examples of dualism in biomedical contexts, explaining how "we have seen that characteristics that are less socially desirable, such as a lower IQ, passivity, and a lack of dominance and aggression (which results in the desire for care rather than the ambition to pursue a career), are ascribed to women" (109). Her treatment of neuroendocrinology and the science of hormones and human brain development shows that cultural ideas about men and women influence the research models and the questions asked. For cancer specifically as Ornella Moscucci explains, "gender ideology informs public perceptions of cancer risk, medical approaches to cancer and the production of various narratives about this disease" (285). Such attitudes about female bodies pervade both Western medicine which moves to Kenya through global medical flows, as well as Kenyan culture, creating a double constraint for Ogola's text. Tom Odhiambo adds that "the obstacles in a patriarchally inclined society like Kenya are beliefs like ones that depict women as the weaker sex, both physically and intellectually" (245). In his article about Ogola's first novel *The River and the Source* Odhiambo suggests that her characters push against these patriarchal beliefs, but through the depiction of cancer *Place of Destiny* recreates and affirms those gendered assumptions.

Men Choose Cancer, Cancer Chooses Women

In *Place of Destiny*, Amor Lore and Igano Magu die of interesting and very different cancers, and those dissimilar cancers and sites become gendered in their presentation. Amor Lore contracts liver cancer, through no clear fault of her own. She explains the staging and site of her disease early in the novel: "I have cancer, extensive and invasive, apparently originating in the liver. It has already spread to the right lung and the abdomen" (Ogola 25). On her first visit to the doctor she reports, "I must say in the good man's favour that he looks, after poking around my abdomen for a good fifteen minutes, genuinely perturbed to discover that my liver is markedly enlarged" (24). She has an internal tumor, close to reproductive organs, but not in one of them. While her cancer does not manifest in reproductive organs, Lore does have a swollen abdomen with the liver cancer. The swelling in her abdomen, similar to the appearance of early pregnancy, connects her cancer back to her capacity to carry and birth children. This manifestation of cancer in non-reproductive organs avoids the suggestion that sexual activity or behavior caused her disease, but the mimicry of pregnancy maintains a certain feminine quality in the disease. A swollen abdomen becomes suggestive not only of reproductive processes but also of obesity or of overeating. Of course, Lore is neither pregnant nor obese, but originating the cancer in her abdomen connects her firmly to those bodily developments, which her swollen abdomen mimics. From what we learn, this markedly enlarged liver does not respond to immoderate alcohol consumption or other excesses. Lore's cancer seems to have no behavioral cause, despite its appearance in the organ whose main functions are aiding in digestion and detoxification, a space where those types of excesses could manifest. Instead, her body is itself the culprit, turning on Lore for what appears to be no reason at all. Amor Lore contracts cancer as a result of fate, and one suspects that her fate of being born female leads to the fate of cancer.

Unlike some characters, Lore does not immediately allow indiscriminate medical intrusion. When her physician initially finds swelling she explains, "Apparently bigger is not necessarily better in medicine, but to tell you the truth I'm not a person too pre-occupied with the goings-on inside me. My view is that if one is meant to know, there wouldn't be such an all encompassing skin" (24). Lore's *laissez faire* attitude toward medicine suggests that she has not internalized the power of the medical field or the ways they might think about her body. Her attention to skin may refer to the importance of skin in understanding health and it may also reflect the importance of boundaries and borders. Like all colonized places, Kenya and its people attend to borders. For them, fears about porousness may have less to do with military invasion fears, and more to do with refugees traveling across the borders from South Sudan, Somalia, and Ethiopia. Their own peace, order, and economy are stressed, while incoming migrants from more tenuous states compromise their growth. For Lore, skin provides an important metaphor for boundaries, and unlike some cancer patients, she is mostly allowed to maintain those boundaries as she grows increasingly ill and then dies. Her skin border is, in fact, crossed mostly when she authorizes it, and at first, she retains the ability to control the setting of those border crossings. This offhand reference to skin appears somewhat flippant. However, given the context of its delivery as Lore receives the news of illness, it may suggest something important about health attitudes. Lore's insistence on the importance of skin as boundary may indicate less acceptance of medical intrusions in a Kenyan context than elsewhere.

Destiny provides encouraging ways of viewing medical personnel, and the health care professionals here are not overbearing or coercive. According to Lund, Western medicine maintains a positive evaluation and elevated status in most of Africa. She explains "to this day, Western medicine and hygiene are widely considered the greatest gifts of colonization; public health is one of the few arenas in which foreign intervention in Africa is usually accorded unquestioned legitimacy" (Lund 163). Ogola's text backs this claim as the narrative continues to represent the medical field in mainly approving ways, especially by disallowing medical personnel overt domination over the patients. Lore, in fact, at the novel's beginning, fights against deferring to the schedule of the family doctor and oncologist, first waiting for her husband to return to get some of the tests and then going on a vacation while ignoring some treatment advice. In addition, Lore never gets incorporated into a hospital facility. She is instead allowed to die at home using hospice care, which suggests a somewhat positive attitude toward the medical field in this novel. The physicians here make no attempt to enclose Lore in a hospital or constrain her movements in real ways, avoiding any villain role. Yet, the changes to her life as a result of treatment become very real as she relies more and more on pain drugs. Ogola's version of medical doctors represents a positive view, and the text never questions the gendered assumptions about women and cancer transferred to Kenya by Western biomedicine, perhaps due to her own status as a doctor.

The male character in the novel dying of cancer, Igana Magu, who contracts a throat cancer due to his smoking habit, receives markedly different representation in the novel. Both the man himself and later the narrator explain how the cancer he contracts relates specifically to his behavior. He claims: "They have sent me here because of this thing in my neck. Cancer. I now know it is most probably because I have been a heavy smoker most of my adult life. But so be it – everyone has to have some way of relaxing and smoking was mine" (Ogola 172). Magu takes responsibility for his illness and suggests that his death was of his own choosing. He has engaged in the riskiest of cancer-causing activities, smoking, and his neck cancer develops from just that conduct, as both character and narrator specify. By contrasting Lore's cancer as fated with Magu's cancer as needing a chosen carcinogen, the text reinforces the idea that men's bodies are strong rather than tending naturally toward disease. Even in a text that creates cancer in a male character, the narrative attributes his death to activity on his part. Men are never just victims of disease; they do not passively acquire cancer. Instead they actively engage in risk-taking behaviors like smoking, which then lead to their contracting cancer and finally to their death. The text attributes cancer-causing behavior to the male cancer patient, and introduces his character after the cancer has been treated and recurred, long after the damage of smoking has occurred. There is no pre-cancer moment for this character in the text, when medical professionals could have provided smoking-cessation advice for him. He might be encouraged "never to smoke again," but the proscription comes after cancer has ravaged his body. The text declines to advocate screening and public health measures aimed at male bodies and takes male bad behavior as a given, a situation that exists before the story begins, suggesting that such behavior will always be a choice for men.

This active, autonomous portrayal of Magu's relationship with cancer contrasts with the development of Lore's disease. In the first section of the novel, Lore learns about her disease, and struggles with the information. She suggests that "I'm forty-nine years old and if am lucky I might celebrate my fiftieth birthday – that is if I manage to stay alive for the next five months. If I do, I'll most certainly be in severe pain by then" (20). Lore describes her possible future with the term "if," repeating the word three times in this short passage. This renunciation of certainty, especially the repetition of "if" counters the finality of "Magu Igana is a dying man" (171) that we hear when Magu is first introduced. Lore qualifies her cancer prognosis and indeed her choices going forward using words of possibility. In the same passage, she uses the word "lucky," again shifting her autonomous choices about life to chance and fate. Magu never includes the word "luck" or "chance" or even "if" in his discourse about his cancer. Both he and the other speakers who describe his disease, including the physician, use discourses of surety and finality rather than the language of luck and probability on which Lore depends when she first learns of her cancer. Magu claims "I now know it is most probably because I have been a heavy smoker most of my adult life" (172). Despite the addition of "probably," he claims to "know" about his cancer and its cause, information that Lore is denied. In fact, for Lore the cancer itself seems to have more agency than expected, when she refers to its growth saying, "And, unless the cancer unexpectedly eats its way into a large blood vessel or something like that . . . I still have those four, maybe six months" (32). While cancer does indeed progress in the ways Lore describes, the active voice "eat its way" portrays the nonsentient tumor her body has produced as exercising agency, when Lore herself cannot decide how the remainder of her life will progress.

Indeed, Lore only once hints at personal responsibility for her disease in the moments when she worries about her husband's or children's ability to cope, but she does not actually believe that her actions have created the cancer. When she first announces the bad news to her husband she reflects "I am consumed with pity for him almost as if I'm personally responsible for being afflicted with cancer" (43). Unlike Magu, Lore does not literally attribute the cells attacking her liver to her own behavior. Her "almost as if" suggests that this idea is foreign to her. Instead, Lore remains an ill-fated victim of cancer, rather than an active agent in its formation, its progress, or its treatment. Thus, the Ogola novel succumbs to one of the biomedical cancer biases, the idea that women's bodies are naturally oncogenic and will develop cancer regardless of whether women engage in risky behaviors.

Amor Lore's liver cancer remains unconnected to deportment or activity; the text makes no mention of excessive drinking on Lore's part or of any hepatitis infection caused by risky sexual or drug injecting habits. *Destiny* confirms a belief that women self-regulate behavior, perhaps because social judgment for smoking and drinking is already more inflexible for women. For Ogola's text, women already adhere to stringent dictates that they comport themselves a certain way. In her Catholic world view, biomedical dictates against excessive alcohol consumption, or against multiple sexual partners may become superfluous.

Like the acquisition of cancer, Lore's treatment options reflect passivity as well. Contrasting with Magu's initial treatment, chemotherapy with "powerful drugs" (185), Lore's cancer is too "extensive" for chemotherapy or radiation from the moment she learns of it. All treatment options are removed, and she has no difficult decisions to make about her health care. The cancer itself instead gets the autonomy and choice. In this way, Lore seems less strong, less autonomous, and perhaps less human than Magu.

Location. Location. Location. Or, What the Sites of Cancer Mean

Interestingly, Magu's cancer attacks his head and neck, not his abdomen. In this way, he becomes much more related to his intellect and subjectivity than Lore. Even his choice to smoke originates in the head, while smoke enters the body through the mouth. His cancer site develops in centers of decision making, rather than from his mid-section. While the neck is not technically part of the head, it protects and holds the head on the shoulders, while also shielding the spinal cord, an extension of the brain. The neck, thus, connects more to thinking and supposed higher functions than the literally lower abdomen, which is the site of digestive and reproductive processes.

In Western thought, mind and body have become separated and placed in a hierarchy. Rather than an integrated intellectual and corporal person, those aspects of humanity are perceived discretely, with the mind taking precedence over the body. We label biological processes base and call humans a higher life form due to our intelligence, suggesting that the mind is nobler than body. As part of this tradition, women are identified with the body, while men are connected to the mind and the spirit. The siting of the characters' cancer places their disease and thus their persons on this mind body continuum.

Magu's cancer also originates from the nose, the space where inspiration occurs – literally where air is drawn in – and symbolically connected to mental or spiritual inspiration as well. His tumor is located in the space behind the nose that allows breath to move toward the lungs, bringing life and ethereal air, reminding us of humanity's ability to connect with the divine. Thus, Igana Magu's nose brings in immaterial air and links our notion of him to his mind and spirit, while the liver, Lore's cancer site, processes material, especially waste. The liver's main functions include aiding digestion and detoxification, linking Lore to base corporeality. This cancer of Magu's originates from what might be seen as an addiction of the body, smoking, but the stuff of addiction converts to ethereal ether, made of spirit. While most clearly a space of immateriality, Magu's cancer site is not solely connected to the spiritual and intellectual, because the nose functions to allow the sense of smell. While it remains part of the head, the nose as space of sensory operation retains a small essence of the bodily and innate. Yet, researchers understand olfactory function as the sense most triggering of mental activity like memory, reconnecting it to intellectualism.

The connection of men with the head and logical abilities manifests in Magu's illness. His designation of cancer in the head and neck, as opposed to Lore's site in the abdomen, again reinforces his connection to logic and rationality. Lore, on the other hand, becomes connected to, if not reduced to, her corporeality. The belly's distinctly bodily processes, suggests less inspiration and more degustation or reproduction. His cancer's location reifies our conception of men as thinking, active creatures, while the liver connects Lore to her body and her animal materiality. Because his illness is in his nose and neck, Magu maintains, despite brief mentions of nausea during chemotherapy, distance from his trunk and his corporeality. Similarly, his rational acceptance of the disease and his thoughtful reminiscences about his own decision to smoke, contrast sharply with Lore's emotional descriptions of her sadness, her relationships to spouse and children, and her human need to come to terms with the disease over time.

It's All About Control

Igana Magu's health prior to his cancer, while in some ways weaker than Amor Lore's earlier health, results in less medical intervention and even his cancer treatment results in fewer intimate details provided to readers. Because of his male status, Magu directs his medical treatment more than Lore, and unlike her, his increasing weakness as the disease progresses remains off stage. To begin, his cancer responds to treatment with chemotherapy for a time, an option that Lore never gets, due to the advanced stage of her cancer. This intervention makes him uncomfortable, but ostensibly extends his life. In addition, Magu admits to a dreaded childhood disease, perhaps connected to his suspected sterility, "I had testicular mumps at fourteen. Probably did the damage. I could never bring myself to undergo any tests" (172). Even though it portrays childhood illness in his body, the passage reports Magu's unwillingness to test his fertility, and it reflects how men are allowed and encouraged to forego medical interference based upon their own choices and their perceived intact bodily autonomy. Men like Igana Magu are encouraged to make their own decisions about their bodies and the care they accept in ways that women, who bear the responsibility for public health as well as reproduction, are not allowed.

A woman experiencing similar suspicions of barrenness could be entreated or even forced to undergo medical testing by her husband. Similarly, some women who fail to produce a child may be divorced or faced with a second wife entering the family. A report on "The Status of Women and Girls in Kenya" suggests that "infertility is a hardship for women, particularly in rural areas, where women are blamed for the condition and often divorced and ostracized as a result" (10). Thus, women have less ability to refuse medical intervention in instances of sterility and other contexts than do men in Kenya.

This narrative gives Igana Magu the chance to own and almost control his death. He explains, "I have lived a very stress-filled life. Now I am dying for it" (Ogola 172). Here again, Iganu suggests that his actions and choices in responding to stress created his fate. This fantasy of self-determination in death provides the male character with even more autonomy than merely power over health care choices. One thing over which most of us have very little control is the time and means of death. Yet, this text cedes influence over death to the male character to a much greater degree than the female character, who seems to die at the whims of fate. This reification of the male=active, female=passive binary builds different ideas about disease for women and men into the narrative, once again suggesting that women do not have – and perhaps should not have – the same autonomy as men. These images of male decisiveness create a fictional world where men can maintain control over their bodies to a greater degree than their female counterparts.

As evidence of the self-determination given to male characters, Magu explains his family situation and describes his and his father's behavior: "We both gradually sank into a fitting state of chronic misery – with my father drinking like a fish and me smoking like a chimney" (185). The text introduces Magu late and reveals only a little of his story; however, his relationship with his father and his choice to smoke figure prominently. This portrayal of misery and self-medication suggests that men bear stress and that they maintain the autonomy to address their stress through any means they see fit. Male characters commit the kinds of abuse to body and health that women are encouraged – and even forced – to forego for childbearing and thus public health reasons. Excessive drinking and smoking always damage the individual's body, but when they present a threat to the body politic in the form of children, restrictions tighten. In this text, only male characters are positively described using substances as stress relief. The narrative allows Magu and his father the autonomy to choose damage to their corporeal persons through ingesting alcohol and tobacco. Although Magu gets punished for his choices, they remain his choices to make.

Subtle messages about Lore's role or place in the world continue at the hospice center to which she gets referred by her primary physician. The other cancer patient characters in the novel who are treated at the hospice center are all children. Magu becomes the only adult male with cancer whom the novel introduces or even describes, and Lore is the only adult female with cancer about whom we get any detail. The text describes one other adult female cancer patient at the hospice center, introduced only once, about whom we learn that she is "in her sixties and is accompanied by a youngish man, probably her son" (102). This woman does not reappear in the text, but she represents a version of the sick elderly body that one expects as the norm in a cancer hospice setting. Perhaps the preponderance of younger cancer patients in the text reflects Ogola's own work with sick children, but it certainly shows which bodies represent illness in the world of the text. Adult men with cancer other than Magu are not revealed in the hospice setting, again suggesting that women and children have the weaker bodies that are more susceptible to diseases like cancer. Also of note in a text written by a woman with medical training, there are no female doctors in the novel.

When Magu enters the novel, readers learn a bit about his cancer: "A sample from the swelling revealed a most malignant throat cancer – or postnasal space carcinoma as the doctors call it. They started me on a round of chemotherapy – powerful drugs that left me feeling half dead and terribly nauseated all the time" (185). Here the text provides the only details about Magu's struggle with cancer except a quick description of the "rubbery masses in my neck" (185). While this first-person description reveals somewhat grotesque details, readers do not see most of the distasteful information about his treatment. His cancer gets very little attention in the text compared to Lore's extensive reports about pain, yellowing eyes, gastro-intestinal discomfort, and weight loss, in addition to changes in her approach to life and to divinity. Because his character becomes less central to the plot, this lack of information about his disease could signal that such detail remains superfluous to the text. Yet, it also suggests an unwillingness to dwell upon the weaknesses of the male body in the same way that weakened female bodies like Lore's are described with lingering detail.

We get much more information about Lore's movement through disease such as description of vitality "ebbing away, anyone can see that the hollow cheeks and sunken eyes tell a tale" (140). Information about her pain management is also forthcoming, and readers learn how "her pain control is now like walking a tight rope. [Dr. Mago] sometimes has had to increase the dosage of morphine. At other times, especially when she wants to be a little more lucid, he decreases it while stepping up the dosage of other types of pain relievers" (140–141). The text describes pain management of late stage cancer in fairly accurate detail, using Lore as its sole example. The information about her levels of lucidity inform readers that her mind is being overcome by pain and medication, a fate that separates Lore further from the mind and correlates her existence with body. This subtle movement along the mind body continuum that Lore experiences and the reader gains access to, never happens to the other cancer patients, although surely they have pain managed by drugs. By explaining how Dr. Mago "confided" pain information, the text signals that medical information usually remains private, but within this reader-text relationship, medical data gets provided about Lore that might not otherwise be forthcoming. Information about these symptoms and treatments is considered private, and through the intimacy of the narrator, readers are allowed into the physician patient interactions. These data bits allow readers to form sympathetic ties to Lore's character, but they also display the cultural willingness to document women's illness in ways that the male characters evade. As Holloway explains "women and blacks – are bodies that begin with a compromised relationship to privacy" (9).[1] Here as elsewhere, the narrative intimately represents Lore's body as weak, giving in to pain and destroying her thinking self, while confiding no such detail about the male patient.

Infantilizing Adult Patients

Finally, the text actually uses the word weak to describe Lore. As she loses her struggle against the cancer, her family eventually moves her from her own bed. In the final days her daughter explains "Mama has become desperately *weak*. . . . Daddy finally agreed to move her to the baby room. It's simply more convenient and manageable. She is too sick to be lolling in that great bed" (Ogola 145). Moving Lore to the baby room both infantilizes her and reconnects her with – perhaps reduces her to – her reproductive capability. As a patient in the baby room, requiring constant care, Lore's ability to care for her physical body has been reduced to that of a baby, and the reader is provided details of that physical diminishment. Additionally, the baby room carries the traces of Lore's reproductive years. She nursed and cared for her four children as they began their lives sleeping in the same baby room. The text again signals that her mind and spirit are not important, but her reproductive body remains key though that body is weak.

The male cancer patient receives only limited health directives and his bodily weakness does not get highlighted in the story. Readers understand that "At the end of four weeks they allowed me home with orders never to smoke another cigarette ever again" (185). As a health imperative, instructing a patient not to continue smoking remains fairly noninvasive, and this advice to stop smoking cigarettes constitutes good general health advice for all humans. Here we have one example of health care officials intervening in male autonomy over his body, but the example remains an extreme case when the cancer is very pronounced and far along. His providers' "orders" only come when his life is endangered by further smoking, not merely as a public health suggestion meant to be followed for the public good or successful reproduction.

Margaret Ogola's final novel provides an opportunity to view broader gendered ideals in the same text with ostensibly insider medical views about health care and gendered bodies. The narrative begins along a feminist trajectory with a character clearly oppressed by the patriarchy, but the premise soon gets undermined by a combination of limiting roles for women – one can be anything in addition to a mother, but one must be a mother – and subtle messages about the weakness and oncogenic nature of female bodies, including the need for medical intervention upon those bodies. The text centers around a woman who does everything right – earns money, bears and raises four children, loves and supports her husband – yet still dies early from cancer. Clearly Lore represents a powerful character, whose presence in the text projects feminist ideals. Evan Mwangi calls Lore "a formidable female character fighting cancer and passing the mantle of leadership to a younger and highly motivated woman" (121). Yet the images of her oncogenic body that accompany her narrative question those ideals, and display how Western notions about disciplining female bodies carry over within capabilities like cancer treatment protocols and chemotherapy drugs. Women's own capabilities can diminish as those notions shift bodily autonomy away from women toward medical professionals. Although the novel presents Lore as exceedingly skilled and competent, this character still epitomizes a physically sick woman. The novel fits into an existing pattern of the oncogenic women trope traveling from Western cultural and biomedical norms into the Kenyan culturescape via global transfers of medical equipment, training, and attitudes.

Note

1. While Holloway addressed the United States, see also Ayo Coly explain "postcolonial African angst over the female body" (13).

Works Cited

Cole, Catherine M. " 'Give Her a Slap to Warm Her Up': Post-Gender Theory and (a) Ghana's Popular Culture." *Africa After Gender?* edited by Catherine M. Cole et al., Indiana UP, 2007, pp. 270–84.

Coly, Ayo A. "Un/Clothing African Womanhood: Colonial Statements and Postcolonial Discourses of the African Female Body." *Journal of Contemporary African Studies*, vol. 33, no. 1, 2015, pp. 12–26.

Gikandi, Simon, and Evan Mwangi. *The Columbia Guide to East African Literature in English Since 1945*. Columbia University Press, 2007.

Government of Kenya. Ministry of Health (undated). *Status of Women and Girls in Kenya*.

Holloway, Karla. *Private Bodies, Public Texts: Race, Gender, and a Cultural Bioethics*. Duke UP, 2011.

Lund, Giuliana. "Dirty Work: Acting Up and Speaking Out, 'Good Medicine' for Africa." *Emerging Perspective on Tsitsi Dangarembga: Negotiating the Postcolonial*, edited by Ann Elizabeth Willey and Jeanette Treiber, Africa World Press, 2002, pp. 161–87.

Moscucci, Ornella. *Gender and Cancer in England, 1860–1948*. Palgrave, 2016.

Mwangi, Evan. *Africa Writes Back to Self: Metafiction, Gender, Sexuality*. State U of New York P, 2009.

Nelson, Nici. "Representations of Men and Women, City and Town in Kenyan Novels of the 1970s and 1980s." *African Languages and Cultures*, vol. 9, no. 2, 1996, pp. 145–68.

Odhiambo, Tom. "Writing Alternative Womanhood in Kenya in Margaret Ogola's *The River and the Source*." *African Identities*, vol. 4, no. 2, 2006, pp. 235–50.

Ogola, Margaret. *Place of Destiny*. Paulines Publication Africa, 2005.

Rinkanya, Alina. "Woman for President? 'Alternative' Future in the Works of Kenyan Women Writers." *Tydskrif Vir Letterkunde*, vol. 51, no. 2, 2014, pp. 144–55.

Shildrik, M. *Leaky Bodies: Feminism, Postmodernism, and (Bio)ethics*. Routledge, 1997.

Strother, R.M. et al. "The Evolution of Comprehensive Cancer Care in Western Kenya." *Journal of Cancer Policy*, vol. 1, nos. 1–2, 2013, pp. e25–e30.

Tuana, Nancy. *The Less Noble Sex: Scientific, Religious, and Philosophical Conceptions of Woman's Nature*. Indiana UP, 1993.

Wijngaard, Marianne van den. *Reinventing the Sexes: the Biomedical Construction of Femininity and Masculinity*. Indiana UP, 1997.

Yieke, Felicia. "Gender as a Sociocultural Construct: A Sociolinguistic Perspective." *Journal of Cultural Studies*, vol. 3, no. 2, 2001, pp. 333–47.

4 Kenyan Healthscapes
Oncogenic Women in the Nairobi Cancer Registry

While Margaret Ogola's novel represents cancer and cancer treatment in a fictional setting, Kenyans address cancer in their globalized healthscape with varied and comprehensive indigenous healing medical traditions as well as a strong Western biomedical presence. Examining the broader culturescape of cancer and cancer care in Kenya reveals two main pathways: global flows of Western biomedicine into Kenya through vehicles like the World Health Organization, and attempts to use traditional medicine to solve cancer conundrums that Western medicine cannot. A number of researchers work across both traditions, using biomedical laboratory testing procedures to isolate the usefulness for cancer treatment of plants used by traditional healers.[1] An analysis of these two avenues for cancer care with a focus on the biomedical incursions may illuminate how Western preconceptions about cancer as a woman's malady may be transmitted into the Kenyan cancer culturescape.

Why Kenya and Why Now?

In the final chapter of their comprehensive study of biomedicalization trends in the United States, Adele E. Clarke et al. address the transnational circumstances of biomedicalization, especially in postcolonial contexts. She requests international research with this exhortation: "But both 'things medical'... and the dynamics of (bio)medicalization travel widely, and we urge scholars to research empirical cases in and across other sites" (380–381). At a crucial moment of biomedical development, Kenya provides the sort of case for which Clarke and her colleagues are calling. Currently, attention is turning to cancer in Kenya, including both oncological research and treatment, as somewhat absent and much needed. As cancer incidence rates rise and efforts to control infectious diseases like malaria show results, including bringing the AIDS epidemic under control, clinicians, researchers, and politicians, as well as outside cancer research groups see an opportunity to better respond to realities of increasing cancer incidence (or at least increasing diagnosis). As a kairotic moment, this border crossing of biomedical procedures, specifically the introduction of tracking through registries, as well as broader attempts at prevention, screening, and treatment for cancer provides a glimpse into biomedical global flows. Cancer registries are a common way for biomedical experts to track cancer incidence and mortality, and Kenya's two newly formed cancer registries bring biomedical strategies (and assumptions) with them into Kenya's medical context. As Clarke et al. see it, "Another empirical alternative, then, is to study biomedicalization in its transnational travels by studying particular healthscapes as traveling assemblages" (401). Their use of the Appadurian term of "healthscape" expresses the concept of biomedicine and its practices as global flows. As a previously overlooked disease in the Kenyan context, cancer's definitions, activities, and attention patterns build from both local and global actors.

The untimely death of Nobel Prize–winning activist Wangari Maathai from ovarian cancer brought attention to cancer incidence in Kenya. As a very public champion of environmental care, Maathai represents a too-young victim (71 years) of a disease that responds at least in part to environmental toxins. Many factors inform newfound attention cancer receives in Kenya, including influence from external groups like the World Health Organization (WHO). By documenting and analyzing the progression of cancer structures into Kenyan culture, researchers have a window into biomedicalization – and the possible transfer of attitudes about oncogenic women – in real time. What had been a disregarded, somewhat unknown illness in Kenyan imaginations, slowly builds into a national challenge. Recent attention to the burden of cancer in African settings by organizations like the International Agency for Research on Cancer (IARC) and WHO highlights attempts to address disease beyond HIV.

As more evidence of Kenya's growing attention to cancer, October is designated cancer awareness month, and Nakumatt, a large supermarket chain, sponsors awareness in a campaign titled "Let's fight this battle together," taking donations for cancer research, and purchasing billboards and other signage (see Figure 4.1). Their effort to battle cancer in Kenya, which they began in 2014 raised 14.2 Kenyan shillings in the 2016 operation. Similarly, certain providers create free screening times for mammography and PSA tests during October. This additional cultural framework seems similar to the types of campaigns that emerge from biomedical contexts in the United States, and follows their example.

Kenya's budding oncological awareness is discernable in the Nairobi Cancer Registry (NCR) first official report and other documents connected to Kenya Medical Research Institute, KEMRI, as well as the *Policy Brief on the Situational Analysis of Cancer in Kenya* prepared for the Departmental

Figure 4.1 Nakumatt "Let's Fight This Battle Together" poster inside Nakumatt supermarket

Credit: Miriam O'Kane Mara

Committee on Health of the Kenyan National Assembly (lower house of Parliament) in 2011 with assistance from KEMRI. The rhetorical strategies evident in these documents, in addition to the transfer of people, materials, funding, and attention provide a view into the biomedical process of building a cancer infrastructure. Using training offered from the US National Cancer Institute in 2000 and support from IARC and WHO, Dr. Geoffrey Mutuma – with the additional help and support of KEMRI Director Dr. Davy Koech and Centre for Clinical Research Director Dr. Monique Wasunna – founded the NCR in 2001. It was one of the first resources for biomedical research in cancer in the area. The registry is a combination of internal and external influences attending to cancer rates in the country and working to reduce them. Yet the NCR and its counterpart in Moi Hospital, the Eldoret Cancer Registry are not a complete cancer tracking system. Although some information about cancer incidence in Kenya as a whole is available partially due to NCR itself, any reported national numbers must be extrapolated by WHO, as there is no national cancer registry. The NCR resource and the smaller Eldoret Registry provide the data for extrapolating national numbers, and the documents they produce are the best way to understand new biomedical responses to cancer in Kenya. In order to understand those biomedical responses, I will explore the rhetorical strategies in the documents to evaluate how they frame capabilities for medical intervention and patient responsibility and compare such recommendations to incidence data. This comparison shows how the documents both support beliefs that cancer is a female malady, acquired passively, in the face of contrary medical evidence, while complicating that individual risk narrative.

Biomedical infrastructure for illness like cancer must attend to ability to provide care, and it must include attention to access – financial and locational – to that care, in addition to enumerating incidence and mortality. In Kenya all citizens who are 18 years of age and earn more than 1000 Kenyan shillings (approximately 10 USD) per month are eligible for government insurance, allowing treatment at a public hospital, but in reality financial difficulty and socio-economic status, as well as location, drives Kenyans' ability to access health care. According to Strother et al. in 2013 "the National Health Insurance Fund (NHIF), which covers a substantial portion of in- patient hospital fees in governmental hospitals . . . is underutilized – in spite of enrollment fees ranging from US$2 to US$25 monthly only 2.7 million (less than 10% of the population) are enrolled" (26). The current number is 7.3 principal contributors and 22 million members including dependents, according to NHIF's information (NHIF "Profile"). Professional and wealthy Kenyans often carry private health insurance in addition to NHIF, and they get their care at high-end private hospitals. Conversely in rural areas, biomedical facilities and professionals, as well as data collection and record keeping, can be difficult to access or completely unavailable, and traditional medicine can be more common.

Traditional Healing in a Cancer Treatment Context

To accurately understand attitudes about cancer, in Kenya, examining both Western biomedical facilities and traditional healing contexts is important. Any study of cancer within the Kenyan context necessitates attention to the indigenous medical and health practices in addition to the Western biomedical pieces of the oncology puzzle. As Clarke et al. explain "Research that pursues aspects of biomedicine in such situations needs to clearly and deeply understand what else is going on and the distinctive local meanings and symbologies of the various approaches to health, healing, illness, and medicine that circulate in a particular site" (383). In Kenya, up to 80% of medical treatments come from traditional healers, especially herbalists. The reasons for this include "the ready availability of these medicines at local village markets and cost of modern pharmaceuticals which is prohibitive to most of the general population" (Tolo et al. 92). Indeed, according to some scholarly and popular sources, sometimes Kenyans seek out herbalists for cancer treatment itself. In this context, useful information would include ways that traditional healers define and treat cancer. Part of the program of KEMRI's Center for Traditional Medicine and Drug Research (CTMDR) includes "rationalization of traditional medicines in collaboration with traditional healers; evaluation of plant drugs using medicinal Phytochemistry, pharmacology and toxicology and, formulation of herbal remedies"; they also document herbal remedies/medicinal plants used by various herbalists and Traditional Herbal Practitioners (THPs) to treat diseases afflicting the population ("Mandates" CTMDR). Studies attend to the effects of herbal remedies on a number of diseases, including herpes and HIV.[2] In addition, one researcher at KEMRI's CTMDR, Dr. Beatrice Njeri Irungu examines extracts for their cytotoxic properties in conjunction with cancer treatment (Irungu et al.). CTMDR uses Western scientific methods to investigate the properties of traditional remedies, placing biomedical professionals in a relationship with traditional healers. However, the center favors Western biomedicine and their researchers are not traditional health practitioners. What is missing, so far, is an attention to indigenous ways of understanding cancer. If the main facility for medical research in Kenya includes a center for traditional healing – CTMDR assists Nairobi residents who wish to connect with traditional health practitioners like herbalists, and they work with governmental and non-governmental groups to both train and regulate those practitioners – it seems important to account for those practices.

Unfortunately, information about traditional healing and cancer in Kenya remains sparse. Much research has been done to verify efficacy of traditional herbal treatments for malaria, and some work has been done with traditional herbs and herpes.[3] But there is scant information about what traditional healers' believe about cancer or the ways they employ plants that might affect specific types and sites of cancers. What little is available needs supplementation to determine attitudes about cancer in the traditional healer community. Zieglen and Lauderdale interview Nandi traditional healers, finding that two of the four participants include "cancer" in the "Conditions Treated" and a third includes "tumours" suggesting that some traditional healers have integrated understanding of cancer and indeed ways to treat it (147). Yet, their study does not focus on cancer or possible gendered attitudes about the disease.

In addition to KEMRI's attention to traditional healing, some medical anthropology work exists, including Kiyofumi Tanaka's study of two tribes – Kipsigis and Gusii – and their traditional medical practices. According to Tanaka "a traditional healer is sometimes preferred due to the belief that some chronic diseases, like cancer, cannot be treated at the modern

Kenyan Healthscapes 67

medical facilities" (41). While complicated and deadly diseases like cancer might seem a natural fit for biomedical interventions, in the tribal communities Tanaka studies, responsibility for treating cancer often falls to the traditional healer. This preference suggests a possible mine of information about cancer attitudes that predate significant biomedical influence, even as cancer is categorized as a contemporary disease and cancer rates increase as Kenya develops. Tanaka goes on to link the preference for traditional healers in the case of cancer to "high hospital bills" (41), which suggests pragmatic economic reasons rather than hopeful or health related motives for turning to traditional medicine in cancer cases. Cancer is not included in his list of common diseases understood by the Kipsigis, but Tanaka includes cancer in a table that lists "choice of Health Providers by Disease Condition," explaining that the Kipsigis chose to visit the traditional healers for cancer, even though they will attend biomedical health facilities such as hospitals when afflicted with typhoid, meningitis, or malaria. Traditional ideas about cancer appear non-existent or extremely limited based on Tanaka's work, and this absence seems important.

Many illnesses and conditions have supernatural or natural explanations in the rural health traditions of the tribes Tanaka studies. For example, to the Kipsigis epilepsy is both communicable and connected to behavior patterns; in Kipsigis culture you can *catch* epilepsy from engaging in certain activities or from contact with other sufferers of the disease. Contrarily, for Western biomedicine, epilepsy ensues from unusual electrical activity in the brain, and its underlying causes range from genetic influences to head trauma; biomedicine would not consider epilepsy communicable, nor would they connect onset to an individual's behavior. According to David Nyamwaya, "among the Kamba, Kikuyu, Gusii, Tharak, Duruma, Digo, Luyia, Luo, Tugen, and Pokot, in both rural and urban Kenya, . . . regardless of place of residence, education and religion, most people hold concepts of health and illness which have two common features. The first feature relates to the recognition that most illnesses have a biological basis" (5), suggesting that behavioral explanations are not completely pervasive or singular. Neither biological nor other explanations for cancer incidence are forthcoming in the recorded traditional medical understandings of Tanaka's subjects. If traditional health practices do not include an explanation, natural or otherwise, for cancer, then explanations for and attitudes about cancer from the biomedical framework might easily become integrated in the local health contexts. Because for some tribes there is no preexisting narrative of cancer's causes or pathways, new biomedical information coming into Kenya has a profound influence. It follows that any gender biases about cancer found in the Kenyan cancer culturescape could be primarily external, entering Kenya through the networks and influence of Western biomedicine.

Interestingly, cancer *treatment* is included in information about the Kipsigis traditions, despite lack of information for its causes. For the Gusii, cancer receives no mention at all, although one might presume its inclusion in the "Natural Diseases Illness Classification," which includes malaria, and pneumonia (Tanaka 13). For the Gusii, illness in this category results from natural causes and should be treated by "modern medicine" or the "herbalist for herbal medicine (13)." The relative dearth of information about cancer in these two traditional cultures and their health practices might corroborate a common belief in Kenya that cancer is a disease of the West brought by the ills of foreign influence, including nontraditional food choices, pollution, and smoking. Other explanations might be available with additional research, and the interpretations of cancer within traditional healing and herbalist communities is an area that warrants further research.[4]

While the medical anthropology studies of traditional healers in Kenya and the ethnopharmacological investigations of medicinal plants used by Kenya's traditional healers are thus far mostly silent on the topic of cancer, there **are** new biomedical efforts that address cancer in Kenya. The focus on communicable and infectious diseases like malaria and the pandemic of HIV have until recently diverted attention and funding away from cancer research in the Kenyan biomedical milieu, but that is changing. Oncology centers, cancer agencies, and the registries at KEMRI and Eldoret all respond to the burden of cancer in Kenya, urging more research, screening, and prevention attempts in the country.

What Is in the Registries

The two IARC sanctioned cancer registries in Kenya, both products of Western biomedical influence, show how cancer is recorded and addressed in the Kenyan context. Other documents like a policy brief on cancer released by the National Assembly (Parliament) supplement the analysis. Cancer registries as "capabilities" create "intermediation between the old and new orders" (Sassen 13) bringing resources for cancer management from Western biomedicine into Kenya's health system. Because "in modern Western societies, gender ideology informs public perceptions of cancer risk, medical approaches to cancer and the production of various narratives about this disease" (Moscucci 285), influx of Western biomedical practices would likely bring those gendered ideologies about cancer as well. Using the cancer registries focuses on the ways that these entities record overall cancer incidence and make contradictory recommendations that may support the trope of oncogenic women by calling for screening and behavioral change while not advocating for similar screening and behavioral change for men when it is supported by the data.

As semiofficial – the data is collected by non-governmental agencies – and location-specific documents that do not limit their focus by bodily site, the cancer registries function differently than medical essays, clinical trials, etc., many of which deal with a specific cancer site such as liver cancer or a particular drug. Comprehensive cancer information, not limited by site, provides a type of cancer overview for a geographic area, which should reflect cancer treatment and prevention priorities based on burden of disease, availability of treatments and screenings, and related factors. In other words, higher incidence or higher mortality cancers such as liver cancer in Kenya, should ostensibly garner attention in documents addressing cancer in Kenya. Cancers like prostate cancer, which have simple screening tests like Digital Rectal Exam (DRE) and Prostate-Specific Antigen (PSA) tests – though PSA tests require a laboratory – might also be expected to receive attention in regional non-site-specific documents. Factors that affect the attention paid to specific cancers can also include preexisting ideas about gender and cancer, since medical research and clinical practice are cultural as well as scientific forms. If undue attention is paid to a particular cancer, it could indicate cognitive bias that allows practitioners to more readily find, study, or prescribe screenings and treatment of cancers in women, due to social factors. As Moscucci argues women's cancers were used to draw public attention to cancer in the first half of the twentieth century in the UK and US, and Kenya thus far seems to follow that model. If that undue attention occurs in a number of documents and venues, the possibility of bias increases.

The Nairobi Cancer Registry lists Kenyatta National Hospital as the main source of information and lists "five other major private hospitals and a number of nursing homes" (Mutuma and Rugutt-Korir 18) including the Nairobi Hospital as the sites where cancer registrars collect data for the registry. Later in the document they acknowledge Nairobi Hospice as another resource for registry data. Their data collection consists of combing through hospital and other facility records. For each cancer case, they fill out a hard copy abstract form, which are all held in binders within the KEMRI NCR office. Information from these abstract forms are entered into a database (CanReg4 software provided by IARC) and cross-referenced to avoid over-counting.

While there is no cancer registry for the entire country of Kenya, another regional registry in Eldoret collects similar information for a smaller population. The Eldoret Cancer Registry collects data on cancer incidence from 1998 to the present, reflecting the burden of cancer in the region for those years, as well as the cancer priorities of the clinicians and researchers. The recording structures are new, and comprehensive cancer prevention structures do not yet exist. Of course, hospitals and practitioners are trained in diagnosis and treatment. There is an oncology department at Nairobi Hospital, for example. Yet, the registry and accompanying reports are an invaluable record of what has been transmitted from biomedicine.

Screenings, Prevention, and Gendered Recommendations

One stated reason for developing cancer registries is to improve cancer *prevention*. The first report of the Nairobi Cancer Registry justifies its creation by claiming that "quality data" can "allow for effective planning of prevention measures, which include screening programmes and cost effective cancer management" (Mutuma and Rugutt-Korir 13). The NCR follows a basic tenet that data collection leads to screening which equals prevention. Of course, collecting data may aid in bringing attention to disease rates, which in turn, could yield government or private research funding for prevention or cures. Yet, critiques of this approach explain:

> Because stopping cancer from developing in the first place has proved so difficult, when speaking of prevention today, most biomedical experts are referring to secondary cancer prevention – the reduction of mortality via the detection of cancer in its earliest and most treatable manifestations. This kind of semantic slippage has been the source of much criticism from activists and others who oppose the ubiquitous rhetoric that 'early detection is your best prevention' on the basis that it misleads the public into believing that mammograms and breast self-exams are somehow "preventing" cancer, not merely detecting it.
>
> (Fosket 335)

In suggesting that early detection is synonymous with prevention, cancer researchers and clinicians justify the attention, funding, and other support they garner by developing better detection and screening tools. Simultaneously they evade the notoriously elusive questions about actual prevention or cures. In Kenya the "slippage" occurs on an additional layer because "detecting" cancer does not always or even usually lead to treatment, as lack of resources both at the individual patient level and at medical facilities can hamper or preclude treatment.

Fosket's analysis of the troubling use of the term prevention can be extended to the ways that such *prevention* efforts get hierarchized in cancer research and policy. Different tests are encouraged, offered in clinical settings or made part of government policy at differing levels of enthusiasm. This hierarchy of prevention efforts has a number of factors including the burden of the cancer for which the test screens, length of time test has been in use, efficacy of test, and cost, all factors, which make sense for evaluating detection tools. Extant tests such as papanicolaou testing and colonoscopy often become routinized in some clinical settings while newer, less established and more expensive tests like genetic screening may be eschewed. However, other factors appear to affect the popularity of screening and testing tools, including the gender of the people being tested. Papanicolaou tests can be the first cancer screening to be introduced into a biomedical system, despite the invasiveness of the test and its potential for false positives and false negatives.[5] The screening program is popular even though it, "subjects women to an invasive procedure that is of questionable reliability, prone to false positive results, and can cause unnecessary anxiety" (Singleton 88). Moscucci reflects how this screening for women came first in the US partially because "the vaginal smear [papanicolaou] gave the [American Cancer Society] an opportunity to keep cancer highly visible and raise its own public profile" (223) and because "in a system of medical care based on fee-for-service contracts, screening was a marketable and profitable activity" (225), in addition to cultural factors encouraging medical screening for female bodies. She names one of these cultural factors "medical discourses linking women, disease susceptibility and cancer" (285). In this sequence of cervical screenings as first to appear, breast exams are often a close second in popularity among cancer screenings. Non-gendered screenings like colonoscopy or male only tests such as Prostate-Specific Antigen (PSA) screening are often introduced later and/or not encouraged at the same rate.

The effect of gender on screening recommendations becomes evident in the first publication of the Nairobi Cancer Registry. In the NCR report colon cancer is listed as a "major cancer reported among men" (Mutuma and Rugutt-Korir 21), but the report makes no recommendation about colonoscopy, despite its efficacy in early detection of colon cancer, nor do the writers make clinical or behavioral recommendations reflecting the effect of diet on colon cancer. The unwillingness to recommend colonoscopy could reflect biomedical realities in Kenya, such as lack of appropriate facilities for the test, but those kinds of limitations are ignored in this report when recommending papanicolaou tests. As in the US, the reports encourage "pathologization of women's bodies and . . . concomitant production of their bodies as ripe for medical intervention" (Mamo et al. 130). For papanicolaou tests, called as they often are "pap smear," they suggest all women 20 years of age present. While they do advocate for PSA and DRE for men over the age of 45, there are no recommendations for screening or behavior change to address the "relatively high and increasing incidence of oesophageal cancer," which occur mostly in men (Mutuma and Rugutt-Korir 21). According to the (US) National Cancer Institute there is no common screening test for esophageal cancer, although there are trials for screening going on in France and elsewhere.

The first report from the Nairobi cancer registry at KEMRI suggests potential avenues where their work could lead to better prevention through the following efforts:

> Hepatoma which is preventable through Hepatitis B vaccination; better management of cervical cancer through screening which allows for early detection and timely treatment; lung cancer which may be prevented by avoiding risk factors such as cigarette smoking, Kaposi's sarcoma through reduced transmission of HIV and early treatment of those infected.
>
> (13)

The writers here identify a number of ways that prevention efforts could lower cancer incidence in Kenya. However, when they make more specific recommendations for action going forward, early screening for cervical cancer vies with breast exam recommendations (despite some evidence that breast exams are not actually useful for detection)[6] as earliest intervention suggested. In the Kenyan context, as elsewhere, the writers emphasize screening for women, especially breast and cervical cancer. For breast cancer prevention, the writers advocate both clinical provider and home breast exams. However, colon and lung cancers are treatable as well, and the same attention to screening is missing in recommendations for those cancer sites. In the US, Karla Holloway reminds us about how these same assumptions about women's oncogenic bodies surface when genetic testing is recommended for women to screen them for breast cancer: "The association of BRCA1 and BRCA2 mutations to prostate cancer stands in contrast to the absence of public attention about genetic testing in men. This is especially apparent when compared to the public attention dedicated to genetic testing in women and girls for these mutations" (83). Even when the tests are identical and provide possible benefits to both men and women, they are encouraged for female bodies and not male ones.

In addressing the most common cancers in men of which prostate cancer is second, the NCR report explains that "local large scale screening of prostate cancer employing Prostate-Specific Antigen (PSA) testing and digital rectal examination is yet to be realized" and goes on to recommend that "these tests be performed annually for men aged 45 years and above," clearly making a recommendation for male screening (Mutuma and Rugutt-Korir 22). Yet, gendered differences remain, as the writers suggest much younger starting ages for screening women. In the same "Discussion" section of the report, the writers relate how "women of childbearing age should have a clinical breast examination by a health care professional once every three years and should perform breast self-examination monthly"

(22). The language of "childbearing age" reveals willingness to use vague, non-medical and potentially troubling terms, which suggest that all women should reproduce, but using the much more specific "45 years" when recommending screenings for men. Mutuma and Rugutt-Korir use frightening language about breast and cervical cancer incidence with phrasing "as early as 20 years" (22), despite their numbers reflecting only four cases of breast cancer in the 20–25 year category out of 419 total incidence, and only three cases of cervical cancer in the age range 20–25 (37). The language about prostate cancer is much less alarmist stating that prostate cancer "affects mainly men from the age of 40 years and above" (21) even though they record one case in the 35–39 age range and 10 cases of unknown age of 142 total incidence (36). While numbers for early age ranges reflect limited cancers in female reproductive organs, incendiary language in the report highlights the outlier instances of early female reproductive cancers, while reassuringly focusing on the average older ages of incidence for male reproductive cancer. Such subtle cues serve to reinforce the assumptions about oncogenic female bodies and justify expectations that young women undergo invasive screenings, while simultaneously allowing men to possibly place their health in jeopardy.

The KEMRI report recommends screenings for women more readily. In their data, there is no breast cancer incidence below the age of 20, and they admit that "although the age distribution . . . of these two cancers [breast and cervical] is mainly spread between 25 years and 74, they are most common among those in the ages between 40 and 55 years (perimenopause)" (22). They go on to advocate "a Pap smear test together with pelvic examination for women above the age of 20 years, for early detection of cervical cancer" (22) despite their own numbers finding cervical cancer below the age of 30 in only six cases of 107 and only one case between the age of 20–25 – no cases below that age were recorded (43). The inclusion of "together with pelvic exam" provides additional evidence of willingness to perform testing on women beyond the scope of the indicated cancer, since pelvic exam is not the preferred screening for cervical cancer, but rather provides visual or tactile evidence on the size and shape of the entire pelvic area, including ovaries, fallopian tubes etc. Additionally, some research suggests that pelvic exams have little clinical value (Henderson et al.). Careful readers might identify at least one incidence of prostate cancer below the age of 45 in their data set, but the recommended age for "early detection" was not shifted lower for men as a result. As the NCR publication demonstrates, biomedical screening recommendations for women are encouraged more often and at a younger age than tests and screenings for men or tests for cancers more likely to occur in men, like colonoscopy for colon cancer.

The NCR publication at times provides examples of behavior as risk factors for cancer, which is useful when they include accompanying recommendations for lifestyle or behavior change. Yet such recommendations are rarely forthcoming for cancers that primarily affect men, suggesting antipathy for requiring male behavior change. As Mamo et al. explain "groups and their shared collective identifications are key actors in biomedical discourse and practice, resisting certain interventions and identifications and selectively choosing others" (124). For example, the NCR report claims that "since cancer prevention is one of our primary objectives, we have a responsibility to advice people on the benefit of simple lifestyle changes as a means of reducing the risk of cancer" (Mutuma and Rugutt-Korir 23), but they do not advocate any public health efforts connected to smoking cessation or healthy eating, despite the connections between those behaviors and oral and esophageal cancers, which are the number one cancers affecting men in Nairobi. The Report states that "dietary changes associated with consumption of highly processed and non-traditional foodstuffs together with poor nutrition and tobacco use are likely risk factors" (21) for esophageal cancers, omitting HPV as a risk factor, despite HPV's connection to esophageal cancers in other contexts. At the same time, the writers eschew any recommendations for public health efforts to combat the very risk factors they do include: nutrition and tobacco use. In fact, the document seems strangely fatalistic in its treatment of cancer in the esophagus, considering its status as a threat to Kenyans' health, albeit more to men's health. By omitting both the information linking esophageal cancer to HPV and by abnegating any recommendations for public health campaigns against smoking, chewing khat,[7] or improper diet as prevention, the writers display the same shyness toward making screening or behavioral health recommendations for men. Even the mention that liver cancer connects to excessive alcohol consumption does not lead to a recommendation for alcohol prevention programs, again possibly because men are more at risk for liver cancer and biomedicine is less comfortable asking men to change behaviors or submit to screening. The only screening recommendation for men in the entire document is the combination of Prostate-Specific Antigen testing and Digital Rectal Exams for men over 45 to address the growing incidence of prostate cancer, while women are offered papanicolaou screening, pelvic exams, and breast exams both at home and in clinical setting at quite early ages. These age differences not entirely based on cancer incidence may be connected to divergent treatment regimens for different cancer sites, but the document excludes discussion of treatment options, making this supposition impossible to verify. Interestingly, no mention of Human Papilloma Virus or the bivalent and quadrivalent vaccines against it is made in the first report of the Nairobi Cancer Registry, published in October 2006, perhaps because Gardasil, the quadrivalent vaccine was only approved by the FDA in June of 2006. The report writers' willingness to screen women and to ask women to perform self-screening at home, such as breast self-examination, suggests that women's bodies are considered more at risk for cancer generally and also more suitable for surveillance and discipline from the health care system.

A focus on personal risk may also undercut movement toward environmental action and policy change for pollution control. The KEMRI report does not advocate for pollution control or other environmental efforts as part of the cancer prevention plan.[8] Beyond pushing cancer prevention into detection and screening tools that are more routinely recommended for and performed on women, the rhetoric of personal prevention shifts the understanding of cancer causes onto individuals. As Fosket details, "Within processes of biomedicalization, social contexts are often obscured in understanding of health and illness as technoscientific definitions come to prevail. In the arena of breast cancer . . . this has meant a focus on the individual body as the source of risk, rather than on the socioenvironmental world" (349). Within this focus on individual bodies in the biomedical attention to cancer, women's bodies are often the sites of screening efforts called prevention, which are actually early detection. The most popular screening tools for cancer include breast exams, and papanicolaou tests, both of which are invasive and uncomfortable, and importantly, must be performed on individual bodies rather than on bodies of water, air quality or other environmental tests for toxins within a region or area. Screening of individual bodies based on biographical risk factors (age, behavioral elements, genetic factors, and of course, gender) erases environmental considerations from our repertoire in the struggle against cancer, limiting budget efforts to control or mitigate those environmental factors. Celeste Condit explains how "the genetic model of medicine specifies that cancer results from the failure of an individual's genes to regulate cell division properly" (126). In addition, such focus on women's "bod[ies] as the source of risk" (Fosket 349) suggest that the women themselves contain carcinogens, or that they are in fact oncogenic.

Government Policy

In addition to the NCR document, the Kenyan National Assembly published a *Policy Brief on the Situational Analysis of Cancer in Kenya* to address the growing recognition of cancer in Kenya, and it follows some of the gender patterns from the KEMRI report. The "overview" within the introduction to the document explains that cancer "is the generic term for a large group of diseases in which cells grow out of control" (Departmental 2), beginning

76 Kenyan Healthscapes

the document with much more general terms to address the political and general audience made up of people not necessarily trained in biomedicine. The introduction explains the risks for cancer as well, listing a number of "external risk factors including tobacco, alcohol, numerous chemical substances, radiation, and some infectious organisms" (2). Nothing about this list links the external factors to gender and neither do the internal factors, which comprise "inherited genetic mutation, hormone imbalance, immune disorder conditions, and some metabolic disorders" (2). In these first few paragraphs, the understanding of the disease appears ungendered. Yet the next paragraph, which runs under a sub-heading about "policy concern" begins to use gendered language to make subtle suggestions about limiting women's choices and curtailing their medical autonomy through routinized screenings and medical interventions.

The introductory section of the *Policy Brief* from the Kenyan National Assembly, includes statistics and other information about cancer from KEMRI and the Nairobi Cancer Registry as well as other sources. Regardless of information that "oral tumours [more common in men] claimed the biggest percentage of victims" in Kenya (3), and attention to alcohol in the section on liver cancer, the writers leap to the prescription that "women who take more than three alcoholic drinks a day increase their risk of Breast Cancer" (3). This observation about women's behavior suggests a willingness on the part of the authors to prescribe health prohibitions for women, but not for men. Despite the known risk factors for oral tumors including smoking, alcohol consumption, there are no exhortations about *men* who take alcoholic drinks or even *people* (mostly men in Kenya) who smoke. Even though women's passive acquisition of cancer remains a salient underlying attitude in the document, behavioral changes for women enter the mix of recommendations. This singling out of women for cancer concern and behavior modification in the introductory section continues in other sections of the document, especially in regards to cancer screening tests.

Beyond the simple prevalence of attention to women's cancers and to screening or behavior modification for women, the language use in the document becomes important for understanding attitudes about gender and cancer imbedded therein. In other words, the *Policy Brief* includes grammatical and stylistic indications about weak women's bodies. This section from the introduction provides examples of those indicators:

> A study by KEMRI (2010), found that of the 2,292 Cancer-related deaths recorded in Nairobi during a two-year period, Oral tumours claimed the biggest percentage of victims. This report also indicates that people who develop a Liver condition called Cirrhosis, in many cases caused by too much alcohol and Hepatitis B and C viruses can

develop liver cancer. The study also states that women who take more than three alcoholic drinks a day increase their risk of Breast Cancer.
(Departmental 3)

In the description of causative agents for oral tumors and liver cancer, gender is removed with the use of non-gendered nouns like "victims," "people." This section of the report does not refer back to the higher number of men who develop oral tumors, nor does it list behavioral risk factors, like smoking, which can increase the incidence of those tumors. In a similar vein, the non-gendered but [more prevalent in men] liver cancer description uses soft language and both blames but also blurs blame by nominalizing, possibly to avoid the necessity for making health recommendations to men. Unlike the agential language about men and cancer elsewhere, the verbs here are less active, constructing men as victims with the verbs "develop" "caused by" and again "can develop" rather than the much stronger "take" and "increase their risk." The phrase "caused by too much alcohol" does not directly indict actants for "tak[ing]" alcohol but rather suggests that the alcohol somehow gets into those cirrhosis patients. Additionally, the amount of alcohol involved remains unclear with the vague language of "too much" which could indicate any amount from two drinks per day to binge drinking. In the liver cancer patients there is no clear accusation based on a discrete number of drinks, and importantly no way to make a recommendation for behavioral change. Finally, liver cancer's connection to hepatitis B and C is not characterized as behaviorally linked, but merely listed as passive risk factors, even though hepatitis B and C can be sexually transmitted or contracted from drug needles.

Yet, the sentence describing breast cancer risk uses an active voice, strong verb "women who take . . . increase their risk," construction, which names the actor: women, and the behavior: *taking* alcohol and the outcome: *increasing* risk. Here women's passive risk for breast cancer is already assumed, and alcohol merely increases it. In the breast cancer example "more than three" provides an exact number after which women's assumed natural propensity to cancer can be augmented. This also makes it clear which health recommendations can be made for women, while leaving little space for similar recommendations for avoiding liver cancer, which affects primarily men. As we have seen previously, women are described as passive – and reflexively at risk for cancer – much of the time, including in medical documents. One situation where women are ascribed action is where there is an opportunity to make screening or behavioral recommendations for women's bodies. While women are still assumed more susceptible to cancer and constructed as weaker bodies that passively acquire or grow cancer, they are also singled out for behavior modification, which

Foucault reminds us "involve[s] a thorough medicalization of their bodies" (146). The suggestion for behavior change in the name of cancer prevention both gestures toward placing some autonomy over cancer risk in women's hands and also undercuts autonomy by asking them to submit to medical proscriptions. In the practice of biomedicalization, women are asked to "transform" their bodies, and biomedicine "exert[s] diffuse yet constant forces of surveillance and control over living bodies and their behaviors" (Clarke et al. 5). The idea that women should drink less alcohol – using active voice for women "taking alcohol" after nominalized language for men – somewhat undermines the assumption that they will acquire cancer regardless of behavior patterns, but disciplining women's behavior through medical requirements beyond the clinic is not new.

The oncogenic women trope returns in the sections about "Lack of Cancer Awareness in Kenya" on page four of the *Policy Brief* when women's cancers become predominant illustrations. To begin, the example given for a broad category complaint that "too many of the cancer cases are not detected early" is "for example cervical cancer which affects quite a large number of women is treatable if detected early enough" (Departmental 4–5). Early detection of "cancer cases" becomes gendered almost immediately. While cervical cancer's "treatable" quality is ostensibly true, other cancers also respond to early treatment. Colorectal cancer responds well to treatment when found in early stages, and there is no recommendation for colonoscopy in the entire report. This is an example of a seemingly non-gendered broad category, "lack of cancer awareness," moving to a decidedly gendered example in which women are encouraged to allow the biomedical system access to their bodies for invasive papanicolaou screening.

Under the "Inadequate Facilities" sections of the document, the first of the factors "that are back tracking the fight against cancer," (3) undue attention to screening women – rather than screening for the highest cancer incidence – returns. The section addresses outdated radiation technology in Kenyatta National Hospital, as well as naming the newer machines and attesting to their high cost. It then states "there is no equipment like Mammograms, while very few members of the public know of pap smear and that treatment is unavailable" (3).[9] Singling out equipment and tests for women's cancers and not mentioning PSA tests as a missing technology here – only two paragraphs after the statement "Prostate Cancer has assumed unbearable proportions" (4) – seems to confirm the ease of prescribing screenings and interventions for women, while being unwilling to do the same for men. The writers eschew mentioning the non-gendered colonoscopy as a missing technology as well. In two of the eight items listed as problems that stand in the way of treating cancer in Kenya, women's cancers and especially screening tests for young women, regardless of symptoms, are used as examples for the perceived "factors that are back tracking the fight against cancer in Kenya" (3). In none of the eight items is a screening test for men or a cancer specific to men used to exemplify the problem. As in cancer prevention elsewhere, the assumption that women's bodies are oncogenic, unruly, and in need of external control appears.

In the conclusion, the *Policy Brief* provides a number of options for ways forward in the determination to "fast track legal and budgetary policy measures to address the rising incidences of cancer and ensure there are proper strategies for prevention and treatment" (8). These include declaring "cancer a national disaster" as well as dealing with "proliferation of pollutants, carcinogen" by placing "stringent measures of firms that produce substances that pollute the air" (9), a recommendation that distances the report from the attention to individual bodies that biomedicalization favors. However, the environmental suggestion does come last and it follows more traditional ideas like "seek[ing] adequate budget line for cancer prevention, control and treatment" (8). Although cancer prevention measures often include screening bodies for cancer based on risk categories, this recommendation focuses more on providing funds for cancer patients.

As a public health document, the *Policy Brief* moves beyond the biomedical attention to internal risk factors to actually advocate attention to environmental factors. It goes so far as to request limits on business interests that pollute cancer-causing substances with "stringent measures" (Departmental 7). Such recommendations surpass gender and oncogenic bodies and provide a more systemic and justice oriented approach to cancer prevention by advocating restrictions on substances and organizations rather than on particular bodies. The *Policy Brief* thus somewhat complicates the easy transfer of Western attitudes. More of this type of cancer prevention and advocacy could counteract biomedical tendencies that recommend screenings for assumed oncogenic female bodies.

The scholarly article emerging from the Eldoret Cancer Registry reflects both similarities to and differences from the NCR. To begin, cancer incidence appears somewhat similar. For example, Tenge et al. report "Among the solid tumours cancer of the oesophagus (10.5%), cervix (7.9%), breast (6.2%), Kaposis sarcoma (5.9%) and prostate (4.4%) were the most common" (10). Like the NCR numbers, esophageal and prostate cancers are highest in men, and breast and cervical cancers are highest in women. Unlike the NRC, however, men seem to be afflicted with cancer at slightly higher rates than in Nairobi, although not the gender distribution reflected in global samples. Tenge et al. explain that "during the period between January 1999 to December 2006 2,699 patients were males and 2,667 were females." The gender distribution is close to even, when according to GLOBOCAN global cancer distribution men's probability of developing cancer by age 75 is 30.1% while women's is 22% (Jemal 73). Even in the developing world men have a 17% chance while women have a 14% chance of developing cancer by age 75 (73). According to interviews conducted with health care professionals, women in Kenya are much more likely to visit health clinics and admit illness, which may have some connection to the incidence numbers.[10] Eastern Africa and Western Africa are the only regions where cancer incidence is higher for women, and in Western Africa cancer mortality is also higher for women, which makes it an interesting context for studying the gender implications of compiling cancer statistics and managing cancer prevention and treatment. The WHO notes:

> "According to the World Bank income groups for countries. . . . High income countries had more than double the rate of all cancers combined of low income countries. Except in low income countries, men have considerably higher rates of all types of cancer combined than women. This exception is probably explained by the high rates of cervical cancer among women in Africa"
> (WHO "Cancer Mortality and Morbidity")

In this part of the world, responding to cancer in women with more attention makes some sense based solely on the incidence numbers available. What makes that burden higher in Eastern and Western Africa, and acutely higher in Nairobi, although not in Western Kenya, if the Eldoret Cancer Registry is any indication, becomes a question for further research by epidemiologists and others. It may be useful to refer to Moscucci's research showing that similar claims were made about the preponderance of female reproductive cancers during early cancer prevention campaigns in both the UK and the US, and that when fuller procedures were instituted, the numbers eventually did not bear out those claims. Considering the West's overwhelming obsession with African reproduction, the attention to female reproductive cancers by WHO, and subsequently by the NCR, is not surprising. Screening for cervical cancer, means you will find cervical cancer. Julie Livingston explains how "cancer is made visible once it can fit Africa's extant public health frameworks, in other words when it is rendered as yet another sexually transmitted disease" (33). It may be that the registries find what they expect to find; until a wider range of stakeholders direct the process, we cannot be certain. In the meantime, perhaps the tendency in biomedicine toward willingness to screen women more when men suffer from a disease at higher rates translate differently in a context where women may actually bear the burden of cancer more. Yet, even the locally high rates of prostate cancer and oral tumors in Kenya do not receive the screening – or behavioral recommendations – that the breast and cervical cancers do. Thus,

Western biomedical influence appears to use familiar tactics to recreate the warrant of oncogenic woman even where women might actually have more incidence of cancers.

The article from the Eldoret Cancer Registry evinces fewer gender biases, possibly because it does not speak to policy makers or make patient recommendations directly. Tenge et al. suggest that "most of the health care providers are ill prepared to effectively recognize and take appropriate measures when faced with cancer patients" (9). The idea that Kenyan medical practitioners do not have the skills or the tools to address cancer adequately appears in documents from both cancer registries. Both seem to indicate that additional attention to cancer in Kenya must be forthcoming soon. The Tenge et al. article remains mostly gender neutral as the total number of cancer incidence displays a gender 1:1 ratio and the screening/treatment recommendations are made vaguely rather than specific recommendations based on gender. For example, they describe "necessary measures" to address the cancer problem "include proper record keeping through creation of an oncology database, enhancing screening activities, development and use of treatment protocols suitable for resource limited settings" (10). While the recommendation to enhance screening activities might indicate a bias toward papanicolaou tests, the lack of specific screening recommendations for either gender creates a more gender-neutral document than those from the NCR or from the Kenyan National Assembly.

Despite a more gender-neutral artifact, the grouping strategy for cancer sites in the Eldoret report still requires analysis. The number of men presenting with penile and testicular cancers seems high, and the even the choice to combine those two very different cancers into a single category remains unusual, as does the choice to combine vulvar, ovarian, and uterine (non-cervical) cancers, which again stem from different sources even if the locations are considered to be connected. Since penile cancers are connected to HPV and testicular cancers are unconnected to HPV, linking them together relates only to site – men's genitalia – rather than to other similarities. Testicular cancer is non-viral in origin and affects younger men. Likewise, ovarian cancer is unrelated to HPV, while vulvar cancer and some uterine cancers can be HPV related. The only connection between these differing types of cancer is the similarity in site – women's reproductive organs/genitalia – and grouping them together represents a more social or cultural choice than a medical one. While the Tenge document avoids many of the pitfalls of Western biomedical bias towards oncogenic women by not advocating more screening for women, in this choice to record cancer incidences of very different cancers together shows that gendered influence still infiltrates the Eldoret Cancer Registry.

Investigation of biomedical documents about Kenya from external Western sources like the World Health Organization (WHO) demonstrates the biomedical bias of focusing on female cancer and shows how biomedicalization moving into Kenya skews the ways cancer is reported and addressed in gendered ways. If the WHO creates a context where women's cancers are the focus, then the Kenya medical establishment may be more likely to replicate that focus as they integrate Western biomedical methods and attitudes into their overall health care and medical research systems. For example, in a WHO document entitled *Human Papillomavirus and Related Cancers (in Kenya)*, the preface allegedly "incorporates the new burden estimates for *all* HPV-related cancers." Indeed, the report does identify vulvar, vaginal, penile, anal, and pharanx (throat) and oral cavity cancers, as well as cursory treatment of benign infection like recurrent juvenile respiratory papillomatosis and genital warts. However, the report executive summary explains it "is intended to strengthen the guidance for health policy implementation of primary and secondary *cervical* cancer prevention strategies" shifting the focus back to cervical cancer rather than all HPV related cancers. While the first edition of the document only addressed cervical cancers, this document is meant to attend to all of the HPV related cancers, and its focus on cervical cancer rhetorically returns women and especially their reproductive organs to oncogenic status.

The section of the HPV Related Cancers report titled "HPV Burden in Men" refers to penile cancer only, omitting anal cancers – more prevalent in men than women – and head and neck cancers, which the report elsewhere states can be related to HPV. Both by focusing on cervical cancer throughout, and by limiting the burden in men to only penile cancers, rather than addressing the other HPV related cancers referred to in the document, this WHO report subtly insinuates that cervical cancer especially and other anogenital cancers in women are the primary concern for biomedical interventions such as vaccination and screening. They include this warning

> Tobacco use, alcohol use, unhealthy diet, and chronic infections from hepatitis B (HBV), hepatitis C virus (HCV) and some types of Human Papilloma Virus (HPV) are leading risk factors for cancer in low- and middle-income countries. Cervical cancer, which is caused by HPV, is a leading cause of cancer death among women in low-income countries.
>
> (WHO "Human")

Cervical cancer is indeed a prevalent disease in Kenya as in the rest of the developing world. However, this report under-fulfills its title's promise, and in so-doing repeats the common metaphor of the oncogenic woman, by severely limiting its analysis of non-cervical HPV related cancers. WHO specifically focuses on cervical cancer in women without thoroughly explaining its link to other cancers in men.

While the WHO report attends solely to HPV related cancer, the internal Kenyan documents examine the larger cancer context in the country, including but not focused on HPV. While the *Policy Brief* quickly details environmental concerns, the NCR report includes no mention of environmental prevention. This oversight provides a space to evaluate where Kenyan contexts intersect with Western biomedical influences. In the public policy document, while biomedical attention to risk within individual bodies, and especially women's bodies reappears, there is a cursory attention to larger forces, that might affect growing cancer rates in this country, what Livingston calls, "render[ing] African publics particularly vulnerable to the carcinogenic fallout of global capital" (33). The authors of the policy document are a public policy researcher and an intern rather than members of the health or medical profession, would have dual factors influencing willingness to look beyond biomedical explanations. To begin, they have not been trained in Western biomedical practices that create a culture where risk connects to primarily bodies. Additionally, in a postcolonial setting like Kenya, which remains a developing country, despite progress towards economic strength, outside influence from neocolonial sources like multinational corporations creates political understandings that frame how they address internal problems.

New Guidelines Follow Old Patterns

As this book was moving towards publication, the Kenyan Ministry of Health issued a policy document "National Cancer Screening Guidelines," which deserves its own extended investigation beyond this cursory treatment. As we have seen in much cancer discourse, the Ministry document relies only on screening for a comprehensive cancer plan. The Foreword states that the guidelines are "based on . . . international best practice and includes cancers recommended for screening by the World Health Organization, namely breast, cervical, colorectal, prostate, oral and childhood cancers" with the caveat that "early detection of oesophageal cancers has also been included in response to the related high mortality in Kenya" (Ministry 10). This attempt to balance biomedical models from outside and Kenyan health realities reflects an awareness that Kenya must make decisions based on their own health care needs and capabilities. Yet, the Kenyan document openly admits that practices come directly from outside sources like WHO, and we see similar focus on cervical and breast cancers in the screening list. This emphasis on female cancers reflects the development of screening programs in England and the United States that Moscucci outlines. It follows patterns we have seen, claiming even as "increasing availability of HPV vaccination *for girls* and the potential for reduction of the possibility of developing cervical cancer . . . does not eliminate the need for regular screening" (41, my emphasis). And while mammogram machines are expensive and less than ubiquitous in Kenya, "mammography is the recommended mode" and "breast self exam (BSE) and clinical breast examination (CBE) . . . are not screening modalities" (Ministry 15). As in US examples from chapter one, machines are granted agency beyond that of clinicians and especially beyond the agency granted to patients.

A quick look at the document also shows unwillingness to screen male bodies, especially when perceived unmanly penetrations might be involved. Despite WHO including prostate cancer in needed screenings, the Kenyan cancer plan suggests "there is no role for mass screening for prostate cancer. Screening for prostate cancer should be a highly individualized decision between a client and his caregiver, bearing in mind the client's values and preferences" (Ministry 15). Male bodies retain the autonomy already granted them by both Kenyan culture and Western biomedicine, allowing them values and preferences when women get no such affordances.[11] Initial analysis of these *Guidelines* reflect continuation of the transfer of Western beliefs about women's oncogenic bodies into the Kenyan health system and provides another glimpse of biomedical efforts that require screening and regulation to discipline female bodies, a pattern we have seen repeated throughout the volume.

The documents from the NCR, the Eldoret registry, and the Kenyan National Assembly as a set create a focus on biomedical cancer attitudes, which display long established ideas about women's bodies and appropriate health care screening and prevention efforts. Like nineteenth-century British surgeons who maintained a gendered view of cancer despite data to the contrary, these biomedical artifacts transmit belief in the oncogenic nature of women's bodies through the way it frames women's capabilities, shifting them into responsibilities for medical interventions. Furthermore, the documents to varying degrees make arguments for screening women's bodies, while they refrain from arguing for similar screenings for male bodies and/or make weaker claims for screening men or screening for non-gendered cancers, especially those that affect more men in aggregate. The NCR documents create the most gendered presentation of cancer and make the strongest case for screening women for particular gendered cancers. Meanwhile, the Policy document on cancer prevalence in Kenya, written by non-medical professionals, maintains the strongest critique of environmental carcinogens, suggesting that biomedicine creates pathways for certain types of prevention arguments – like the genetic model – and somewhat precludes other types of prevention solutions, while non-biomedical approaches examine broader causes and solutions. Examining how cancers are categorized, which are studied more or less, and which screening programs are developed first can build understanding of gender preconceptions in a cancer culturescape.

Notes

1. See Ochwang'i et al. "Medicinal" and Ochwang'i et al. "Cytotoxic." See also Irungu.
2. See Tolo and Rukungu. See also Orwa et al.
3. Interestingly, a number of plants at the Nairobi Giraffe Centre, sponsored by the African Fund for Endangered Wildlife, are labeled with traditional healing uses, including cancer treatment. The label on the Mytenus Senegalensis or confetti tree suggests "medicinal use" including "cancer suppression" and "snake bite treatment" (Giraffe Centre).
4. In a later chapter I interview a traditional healer as part of a larger sample of Kenyan health care professionals.
5. False negatives average 20–25%. See Flores et al. (262). See also Singleton et al. and Singleton and Michael, who address flaws in the UK cervical screening program including oft-ignored pain involved in collecting cervical samples.
6. See Thomas et al.
7. Users chew leaves of the catha edulus plant, which act as a stimulant.
8. IARC recognizes external pollutants as carcinogenic risk factors, including a 2012 press release (#213) recognizing diesel engine exhaust as a contributing factor in lung cancer. "IARC: Diesel Engine Exhaust Carcinogenic."
9. In the years since the report was written papanicolaou tests – or easier replacement VIA VILI tests – as well as mammogram machines have become more widely available in Nairobi, if not throughout Kenya.
10. See Chapter 5 for interview data.
11. See Mara in Frost and Eble for extended treatment of autonomy for men in the face of prostate screening.

Works Cited

Clarke, Adele et al. *Biomedicalization: Technoscience, Health, and Illness in the U.S.* Duke UP, 2010.

Condit, Celeste. "Women's Reproductive Choices and the Genetic Model of Medicine." *Body Talk: Rhetoric, Technology, Reproduction,* edited by Mary M. Lay et al., U of Wisconsin P, 2000, pp. 125–40.

Departmental Committee on Health, Department of Research, Republic of Kenya National Assembly. "Policy Brief on the Situational Analysis of Cancer in Kenya." Feb. 2011.

Flores, Yvonne et al. "HPV Testing for Cervical Cancer Screening Appears More Cost-Effective than Papanicolaou Cytology in Mexico." *Cancer Causes & Control*, vol. 22, no. 2, 2011, pp. 261–72.

Fosket, Jennifer Ruth. "Breast Cancer Risk as Disease: Biomedicalizing Risk." *Biomedicalization: Technoscience, Health, and Illness in the U.S.*, edited by Adele Clarke et al., Duke UP, 2010, pp. 331–52.

Foucault, Michel. *The History of Sexuality*. 1st American ed. Pantheon, 1978.

Henderson, J.T. et al. "Routine Bimanual Pelvic Examinations: Practices and Beliefs of US Obstetrician-gynecologists." *American Journal of Obstetrics and Gynecology*, vol. 208, no. 109, 2013, pp. e1–e7.

Holloway, Karla. *Private Bodies, Public Texts: Race, Gender, and a Cultural Bioethics*. Duke UP, 2011.

IARC. "IARC: Diesel Engine Exhaust Carcinogenic." Press Release no. 213, 2012, www.iarc.fr/wp-content/uploads/2018/07/pr213_E.pdf

Irungu, Beatrice N. et al. "Constituents of the Roots and Leaves of Ekebergia Capensis and Their Potential Antiplasmodial and Cytotoxic Activities." *Molecules*, vol. 19, no. 9, 2014, pp. 14235–46.

Jemal, Ahmedin et al. "Global Cancer Statistics." *CA: A Cancer Journal for Clinician*, vol. 61, no. 2, 2011, pp. 69–90.

Livingston, Julie. *Improvising Medicine: An African Oncology Ward in an Emerging Cancer Epidemic*. Duke UP, 2012.

Mamo, Laura et al. "Producing and Protecting Risky Girlhoods." *Three Shots at Prevention: The HPV Vaccine and the Politics' of Medicine's Simple Solutions*, edited by Keith Wailoo et al., The Johns Hopkins UP, 2010, pp. 121–45.

"Mandates & Core Values." Centre for Traditional Medicine & Drugs Research (CTMDR). *Kenya Medical Research Institute (KEMRI)*, 2019, https://kemri.org/index.php/ctmdr-collborations?limit=2&start=2. Accessed 11 Mar. 2019.

Mara, Miriam. "Bras, Bros, and Colons: How Even the Mayo Clinic Gets it Wrong Gendering Cancer." *Interrogating Gendered Pathologies*, edited by Michele Eble and Erin Frost, Utah State UP, forthcoming 2020.

Ministry of Health, Kenya. "Kenya National Cancer Screening Guidelines," 2018.

Moscucci, Ornella. *Gender and Cancer in England, 1860–1948*. Palgrave, 2016.

Mutuma, G.Z., and Anne Rugutt-Korir. "Cancer Incidence Report." Nairobi Cancer Registry, *Kenya Medical Research Institute*. Nairobi, 2000–2002.

National Hospital Insurance Fund (NHIF). "Profile," www.nhif.or.ke/healthinsurance/uploads/NHIF_Profile.pdf

National Hospital Insurance Fund (NHIF). www.nhif.or.ke/healthinsurance/home

Nyamwaya, David. *African Indigenous Medicine: An Anthropological Perspective for Policy makers and Primary Health Managers*. African Medical and Research Foundation, 1992.

Ochwang'i, et al. "Cytotoxic Activity of Medicinal Plants of the Kakamega County (Kenya) Against Drug-Sensitive and Multidrug-Resistant Cancer Cells." *Journal of Ethnopharmacology*, vol. 215, 2018, pp. 233–40.

———. "Medicinal Plants Used in Treatment and Management of Cancer in Kakamega County, Kenya." *Journal of Ethnopharmacology*, vol. 151, no. 3, 2014, pp. 1040–55.

Orwa, J.A. et al. "The Use of *Toddalia asiatica (L)* Lam. (Rutaceae) in Traditional Medicine Practice in East Africa." *Journal of Ethnopharmacology*, vol. 115, 2008, pp. 257–62.

Rukunga, G.M. et al. "Evaluation of the HIV-1 Reverse Transcriptase Inhibitory Properties of Extracts from Some Medicinal Plants in Kenya." *African Journal of Health Sciences*, vol. 9, nos. 1–2, 2002, pp. 81–90.

Sassen, Saskia. *Territory Authority Rights: From Medieval to Global Assemblages.* Princeton UP, 2006.

Singleton, Vicky. "Stabilizing Instabilities: The Role of the Laboratory in the United Kingdom Cervical Screening Programme." *Differences in Medicine: Unravelling Practices, Techniques, and Bodies*, edited by Marc Berg and Annemarie Mol, Duke UP, 1998, pp. 86–104.

Singleton, Vicky, and Mike Michael. "Actor-Networks and Ambivalence: General Practitioners in the UK Cervical Screening Programme." *Social Studies of Science*, vol. 23, no. 2, 1993, pp. 227–64.

Strother, R.M. et al. "The Evolution of Comprehensive Cancer Care in Western Kenya." *Journal of Cancer Policy*, vol. 1, nos. 1–2, 2013, pp. e25–e30.

Tanaka, Kiyofumi. "Medical Anthropological Study in Western Kenya and its Implications for Community Health Development." *International Development Center of Japan*, Mar. 2000.

Tenge, C.N. et al. "Burden and Pattern of Cancer in Western Kenya." *East African Medical Journal*, vol. 86, no. 1, Jan. 2009, pp. 7–10.

Thomas, D.B. et al. "Randomized Trial of Breast Self-examination in Shanghai." *Journal of the National Cancer Institute*, vol. 94, 2002, pp. 1445–57.

Tolo, Festus M. et al. "Anti-viral Activity of the Extracts of a Kenyan Medicinal Plant *Carissa edulis* Against Herpes Simplex Virus." *Journal of Ethnopharmacology*, vol. 104, 2006, pp. 92–99.

World Health Organization (WHO). "Human Papilloma and Related Cancers (in Kenya)." 2008, http://s3.amazonaws.com/zanran_storage/www.who.int/ContentPages/82032616.pdf

———. "WHO Traditional Medicine Strategy 2002 – 2005." World Health Organization, Geneva, 2002. WHO/EDM/TRM/2002.

Zieglen, Carol Cathleen and Jana Lauderdale. "Nandi Traditional Healers: Sentinels in an Underserved Environment." *Journal of Cultural Diversity*, vol. 23, no. 4, 2016, pp. 144–51.

5 Kenya's Health Professionals Speak
Attitudes About Cancer in the Field

After analyzing cultural artifacts and documents that address cancer incidence and care in Kenya from the Nairobi Cancer Registry (NCR), Eldoret Cancer Registry, and the Kenyan Parliament; asking health workers about how they understand cancer incidence and suffering reveals how local and global biomedical attitudes commingle and circulate in the culturescape. This chapter reports the methods and results of data collection in Kenya interviewing Kenyan health care providers (HCP). Despite a variety of unexpected responses and themes, much of the participant responses reflect how understandings of cancer in Kenya follows both Kenyan cultural patterns including self-described "patriarchal" ones, and external priorities from Western agencies like the World Health Organization (WHO); the results additionally support how both of these configurations reflect gender preconceptions. Participant answers reify patterns of belief that cancer is a predominantly female disease that women acquire naturally. Western cancer technologies, training, equipment, and medicine move into Kenya as capabilities "wearing . . . the same old clothes" (Sassen 8) of gender beliefs about cancer, and Kenyan HCPs enact the beliefs perhaps because their own culture maintains some negative ideas about women's bodies. Thus cancer care in Kenya is influenced by the ways that local culture and global biomedicine are gendered. Additionally, the findings expose ideas about agency and autonomy as individual capabilities. The practice of health and medicine adds agency both to clinicians, who daily make care decisions, and to patients, who in theory gain the ability to prolong or add value to their lives. Yet agency itself gets gendered differently.

Methods

After receiving augmented international IRB approval from a university review board and additional approvals through the internal Kenyan Fulbright process, and from individual institutions within Kenya, 31 medical

Kenya's Health Professionals Speak 89

professionals participated in interviews or otherwise answered questions.[1] Participants at multiple health care sites, including private hospitals and oncology clinics, agreed to participate after viewing the informed consent document, and did not sign anything because a signature would create identifiers where none otherwise existed (Figure 5.1). The interview questions built from a research instrument with specific questions, but interviews included follow-up queries and digressions. The instrument itself includes questions that collect quantifiable data, as well as open-ended questions that garner qualitative data (see Appendix 1). While five of the participants chose to write answers on a copy of the instrument rather than be interviewed, the remaining semi-structured interviews were recorded both by a researcher

Figure 5.1 Hospital triage and phlebotomy room from research site
Credit: Miriam O'Kane Mara

writing answers and via voice recorder for audio files. Handwritten files by participants were transferred to typewritten files. The audio files were transcribed and the transcription and typewritten files were originally hand coded and then coded using Dedoose software, while quantitative responses were analyzed using SPSS.

The coding scheme developed primarily from codes that emerge directly from the data with some codes corresponding to the literature in the field and previous research. As transcribed interviews were coded, several themes emerged including challenges for cancer care in Kenya (see Appendix 2). As challenges of treating cancer in the Kenyan context emerged as a theme, Kivuti-Bitok et al.'s 2013 article "An Exploration of Opportunities and Challenges Facing Cervical Cancer Managers in Kenya" became salient and helped articulate categories from which the challenge codes developed; additionally the "Inadequate Facilities" sections of the Department Committee on Health policy brief aided in completing these challenge codes.[2] Beyond challenges, another recurring theme was agency or autonomy; many of the participants referred to agential reasons for developing cancer as well as agential ways for patients and HPC to respond to a cancer diagnosis. It was surprising the amount of agency that participants wanted to cede to patients *after* diagnosis, perhaps because treatment can be difficult to access in Kenya. Thus a number of codes develop around agency and passivity. This chapter will report findings from the interviews and written answers from participants.

Women Get Cancer and Men Eschew Health Care

One very gendered pattern the data reflected came from the initial six questions of the interview. The research instrument included paired quantitative and qualitative questions, such as "Who gets cancer the most, men or women" paired with "How do you make sense of that." In this way, the instrument attempts to gather some quantitative data in addition to qualitative data for coding. Participants answered question 1 "who gets cancer the most: men or women?" with women by 71% (see Figure 5.2). Some participants would not choose a category and stated "both," and none of the participants chose a non-binary gender identity. This tendency was repeated in question 3 when participants suggested that women suffer more from cancer than men 80% of the time (see Figure 5.3). Yet they answered question 5, who is more likely to die from cancer, with men 39% of the time (see Figure 5.4).[3]

To begin, these participant answers appear incongruous because patients cannot expire from cancer without first contracting cancer. Yet such replies that women are more likely to develop cancer – in their suggestion that

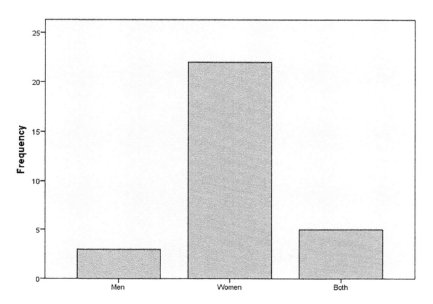

Figure 5.2 Who gets cancer the most

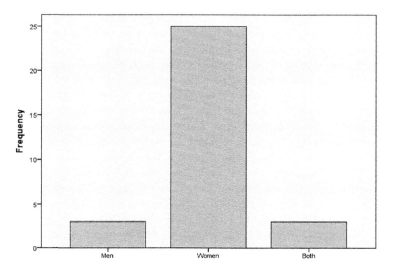

Figure 5.3 Who suffers the most from cancer in Kenya

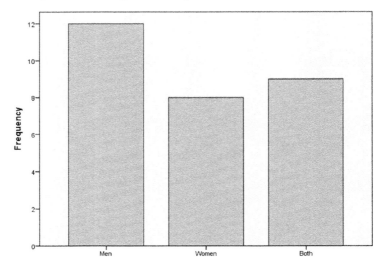

Figure 5.4 Who is most likely to die from cancer in Kenya

women are *naturally* prone to cancer – match observations from Tammy Duerden Comeau and Ornella Moscucci that historically cancer was gendered female in England. Such responses also correspond with Margaret Ogola's novelistic portrayal of cancer as endemic to female bodies, whereas men only get cancer through agential choices like smoking. When respondents indicate that women suffer with cancer more than men, they might reflect embedded ideas about higher pain thresholds or stoicism in men similar to Western biomedical biases that "women are more susceptible to cancer because of some inherent design fault" (Moscucci 2), although some participants would cite women's responsibilities to the family as intensifying their suffering. To better understand this shift from women being more vulnerable to cancer to men being vulnerable to death from cancer, there is useful information in participants' responses to questions 2, 4, and 6, which ask "how do you make sense of" answers to 1, 3, and 5. In answering those open-ended questions, two patterns emerged. The first is that participants connect cancer incidence in women to specific bodily sites, especially reproductive sites, more than they connect cancer in men to specific sites. The other pattern shows that a code for gender-specific cultural differences, appears with frequency in responses about why women get and suffer from cancer more and why men die more. The code reflects when a participant describes something particular to Kenyan culture and gender; it appears for question 2 eight times, for question 4 14 times, and for question 6 eight times, suggesting that culture and gender are lenses through which Kenyans understand cancer incidence, suffering, and mortality.

While respondent answers for this cluster of questions include gender-specific cultural differences, participants answered question 2 primarily with siting language. Question 2 elucidates participant responses about who gets cancer, to which respondents had replied women 71%, and there were 14 instances of applying the siting code here. This pattern of talking about women in terms of cancer sites – breast and cervical most often – matches a Western pattern of reducing women to bodies and to parts. We see this tendency especially in print advertising where women's images reflect partial body parts, often without heads, while whole men are shown, but also in cancer awareness campaigns like Save the TaTas.[4] This siting language corresponds correctly to the types of cancer that primarily affect women in Kenya; yet, the immediate effect of this attention to siting displays attitudes about female reproductive organs as objects rather than larger issues of health, cancer, or women as patients or whole humans. Conversely, the answers to question 6 – "what do you think about [who is more likely to die]" – mentions siting nine times, five fewer than in the responses referring to women. The sites referred were often prostate but once in a while the esophagus, which is not an exclusively male body part. Participants referred to female cancer sites of breast and cervix, sometimes ovarian more than male sites more often throughout.

Rather than siting, in these early questions, the participant more often connects the phenomenon of male cancer, specifically mortality, to a gender related cultural difference, often the cultural expectation that Kenyan men eschew health care. For the follow-up question 6 to "Who is most likely to die from cancer," which they answered men almost 40% of the time, two of the codes applied the most often were gender-specific cultural difference (eight times) and patient challenges. One participant suggests men are likely to die "because men don't talk about it. They just go down with the problem. But women they share and they get psychological support. A man is diagnosed, he just goes down." Here Kenyan men are represented as managing a cancer diagnosis in detrimental ways or giving up. Yet, unhelpful emotional reactions were only part of the explanation, 12 of question 6 answers were coded with patient challenges sub-code of presenting in late stage. In reality, later stage diagnoses are more likely to end in death. Here the participant exemplifies later stage presentation as a gendered cultural phenomenon: "So when they come, it's between [stage] three and four which is not good. But women will come even in stage one." This kind of response to question

6 reflects a cultural commonplace in Kenya that men avoid health care. As we have seen in Chapter 1, the expectation that women present for health care screenings early and often while men maintain complete bodily autonomy both puts men at risk for undiagnosed disease and reifies expectations that women's bodies should be disciplined by others. Suggesting that men decide both to avoid care and to give up in the face of disease indicate that participants saw men's health care behaviors as part of the reason they are more likely to die:

> Even though you don't find so much cancers in men, you find that men have very poor coping mechanisms when it comes to dealing with the cancers when they are hit hard. At the same time, because of the poor relationship they have built over the years, they don't have a strong social support. And they get so angry. They bargain so much with life. And they get a lot of depression.

Presenting in late stage and "going down" are to at least to a small degree behavioral choices that men make. Thus even the participant observations about men as more likely to die ironically connect to agency for men. While participants attribute women's alleged propensity to develop cancer to reproductive parts of female bodies that they represent as inherently oncogenic, they attribute men's alleged likelihood to die from cancer to their decisions and behaviors, ceding a particular kind of autonomy to men, while highlighting women's compliance with health care directives as their capability horizon. Yet, men's autonomy manifests as a loss of the capability to care for their own health.

In addressing who suffers most, to which they answer women 80%, participants use the gender-specific cultural code 14 times. They reflect upon the patriarchal nature of Kenyan culture and the plight of rural women who do much of the farming and household work but have little access to economic independence. One participant who invokes gender related cultural difference explains women's suffering "because in rural communities, women tend to really like hold the family together by taking care of the children and farming and things like that. So, when the lady gets cancer, it really takes a huge blow on the family finances and getting food." Another participant answering question 4 explains that

> You find that social support is very poor, when it comes to supporting a woman, even from her partner. You find that a woman has secondary status especially in the rural areas. They are just treated like objects. They are treated like servants, who will not raise a voice. Majority of them are helpless financially, such that even seeking that health care

becomes an uphill task. And when they fall sick, we find that if she is not helped by the children, actually the partner comes as a last resort.

In addition, participants report that women who become terminally ill are left by husbands, whereas men can expect support and nurturing from wives: "more often than not, if a woman gets cancer and it affects her from doing her normal duties, the husband might marry again. But the husband is supported by the woman even there." Early detection becomes more crucial for women whose partners seem to value them for the work and children their bodies produce and who may leave them if they find late stage cancer. The fact that participants reflect upon their answers about incidence, suffering, and mortality of cancer with responses related to gender-specific cultural differences begins to trace the complex relations between medical realities and cultural beliefs and practices, especially in relation to gender.

Men Retain Multiple Forms of Agency While Women Have Limited Autonomy

Gender again becomes important in recognizing the contrasting autonomy granted to women and men in answers about what causes cancer. As we see in the connections between quantitative questions and the codes found in follow-up responses, the data reflects salience for both where the codes appeared – in response to which questions – and in how often certain codes were used. For the entire data set, the most used code was siting, as participants mentioned siting language 124 times.[5] Such findings partially reflect how HCP use siting to describe cancer and communicate about prevention, screening, and treatment within the context of siting, a biomedical commonplace which likely itself deserves additional analysis. Interestingly, the code used the most after siting was agential causes with 96 mentions. The agential cause code indicates when participants describe behaviors that increase cancer risk, while passive causes reflect risk unrelated to behavior. These concepts about agential and passive causes of cancer were expected to appear based on cultural representations of cancer, especially in Margaret Ogola's novel *Place of Destiny*. In Ogola's novel, men were afforded agency by representing a male cancer diagnosis as the result of behavior (smoking), while the woman in the novel develops cancer passively. Twenty-six of the 31 participants responded at some point in ways that were coded for agential causes. This code occurs with question 15 "What are the causes of cancer in women" the most at 22 times and with question 16 "What are the causes of cancer in men" next, 18 times. This repetition of discourse that reflected agency suggest that for Kenyan professionals who spoke with us, cancer incidence remains somewhat connected to patient behavior.

In question 15, cancer causes in women, the code for agential causes was applied 21 times (by 18 participants), a surprising number if previous texts and contexts suggest women's cancers would be attributed primarily to passive causes. Indeed, the participants invoked passive causes for women's cancers 18 times confirming that the idea that cancer in women can be passively acquired. Yet, they spoke about agential causes more for women than men. They used vague terms like "lifestyle" eight times and sexual behaviors often as well, using language like "multiple partners" or more baldly "sex." Participants also volunteered a connection between use of hormonal contraception with breast cancer, sometimes linking hormonal contraception to Western NGOs: "we have a lot of interventions especially from NGOs, American ones, and family planning methods especially, the forecast or the target groups are usually women in the child bearing ages." A few of the participants described cervical cancer with observations such as "mainly it's cancer of the cervix because of Human Papilloma Virus," which is consistent with current biomedical understanding of many cervical cancers originating from HPV. Some also frame this information in moralistic terms, which fits a familiar narrative.[6] A respondent noted that having multiple sexual partners is connected to HPV, and another followed "Human Papilloma virus. That is HPV" with "prolonged use of hormonal contraceptives" noting "these organs are *meant to* carry babies" (my emphasis). Suggesting that sexual behaviors like use of contraception, numbers of partners – or even contracting a virus that can be transmitted[7] during sexual acts – are problematic or immoral conduct that connect with or cause cancer diagnoses, was one of the few ways that female cancers were attributed to behavior. As Julie Livingston argues cancer's "visibil[ity]" in Africa depends upon making its framing acceptable, and Westerners think of public health on the continent primarily in terms of HIV, a "sexually transmitted disease" (33). Her framing of the problem with cancer in Botswana somewhat matches these findings that HCP sometimes frame cancer in female bodies, as sexual in nature. It matches a tendency in Western biomedicine to frame women's health primarily in terms of their sexual and reproductive health and ability. For example, we have seen how pinkification creates outsize fear of breast cancer in US women, in contradistinction to higher mortality from heart disease. Other examples include how biomedicine creates a specialization in gynecology, and insurance companies allow women to name gynecologists rather than general practitioners as primary care providers. These HCP answers including agential causes suggests that women are allowed more agency than we might expect in the context of blame for cancer. Yet it matches the patriarchal expectation that women's behavior is only important in terms of sexual behavior. In other words, the only agency important for judging women is sexual agency.

Unlike for women, Kenyan participants afforded men multiple forms of agency in acquiring cancer. For question 16 "what are the causes cancer in men" the agential causes code appears 14 times with the majority addressing smoking and alcohol consumption, and men were accorded multiple forms of agency in acquiring cancer. Thirteen of the respondents specifically mentioned alcohol and smoking (cigarettes), and one mentioned chewing khat in answering question 16, "What causes cancer in men," compared to not one mention of alcohol or smoking for question 15 about cancer in women. However, one participant in answering question 16 admitted, "Oh and also smoking, isn't it? Smoking is a cause in both of them I think" linking smoking to cancer in women as an afterthought. While cigarette smoking rates are higher for men in Kenya, smoking's relation to cancer risk does not accrue only to men. These examples reflect that cultural tendencies to attend to a larger set of behaviors when speaking about male agency and to attend solely to sexual behaviors when speaking of women. As in many cases a participant includes multiple reasons in their response: "Predisposition. Cancer has causes from predisposition. I think we can say sedentary lifestyle. And also exposure to bad habits like heavy smoking, drinking." This participant leads with passive causes like predisposition and moves quickly to include three agential reasons for cancer in men, including sedentary lifestyle. This response exhibits one of the few times that "lifestyle" receives a modifier, this participant explains the vague lifestyle moniker with the adjective "sedentary." It may be that in other examples when participants relay "lifestyle" as related to cancer incidence, that they mean sedentary habits, but here, the participant specifies. As with this participant "lifestyle" comes up in question 16 about causes of cancer in men, but only once does sexual activity apply. Another participant suggests that men acquire "prostate cancer for the same reason. They are sexually active." While there is no known connection between multiple partners and prostate cancer, the idea that sexual behavior affects male cancers occurs only this once. For women, as we have seen, sexuality is the main agential cause attributed to cancer risk. Despite the attribution of cancer to agential causes in question 15, smoking and alcohol behaviors were not the agential culprits for women. For men, however, these kinds of agency and bodily autonomy, choices that men make even in the face of risk and danger, were afforded.

While applying agential reasons for cancer incidence to men and women seemed unexpected, participants did follow an expected pattern by indicating passive reasons for cancer in women more often than for cancer in men. For passive causes participants were likely to mention infections, viruses, and environmental toxin exposure, like chemical use on crops, a context that arose a number of times. This willingness differs from tendencies "within processes of biomedicalization, [where] social contexts are often obscured in understanding of health and illness as technoscientific. . ., a focus on the individual body as the source of risk, rather than on the socioenvironmental world" (Fosket 349).[8] One participant included sun exposure as a passive cause for skin cancer, explaining that rural farm workers might spend 12 hours in the fields often without sunscreen and protective clothing. Because respondents addressed genetic risk a number of times, a sub-code for genetic causes was added. Use of the passive causes code in answers about cancer's origin better matched our expectations of gender disparity, as participants used passive causes more for women than men. Participants answer question 15 "What causes cancer in women" with responses invoking the passive causes code 18 times, while passive causes code was invoked only 14 times when participants answered "what causes cancer in men." Participants invoked the sub-code genetic causes similarly in women and men, eight and seven times. Yet, by invoking passive causes more for women, participants reflected the common attitude that women can acquire cancer passively, and that their bodies turn cancerous without introduction of risky, cancer-producing behaviors. The disparity shows that even while medical professionals are aware of the genetic and chance related realities of cancer for all humans, they still attribute cancer in women to passive causes more often.

The attitude about women's susceptibility to cancer even stretched into participant answers ostensibly about men. In answering question 16 about what causes cancer in men, participants sometimes returned to discussing female cancers. One participant when asked about cancer in men begins recognizably with diet as an agential cause and moves into other less expected responses claiming, "Same thing. Mainly diet and obesity. There is infection which is a contributing factor. Mainly its cancer of the cervix because of Human Papilloma Virus. Liver because of the HBV" the participant mixes both agential causes like eating habits with infections like hepatitis B. For this study, infections like HPV and HBV were coded passive causes, unless the participant specifically referred to behaviors that increase risk for those viruses, because both viruses have multiple routes of transmission. This participant returns to cervical cancer, clearly a female reproductive cancer, in their answer about what causes cancer in men. Answering a question about cancer in men, the participant invokes female reproductive cancers, perhaps hinting at the complexity and the persistence of the idea that cancer is a woman's disease. This willingness to focus on female cancers might indicate the level to which some HPC associate cancer with women and especially with women's reproductive organs.

Women's Bodies Should Be More Available for Screening

Beyond passive acquisition of cancer, an additional expression of belief in women's proclivity to cancer reflects in the expectation that women should be more available for medical testing than men and that women's bodies are understood as bearing the burden of society's health care. As Mamo et al. explain "girls and women are primed to receive health care products and messaging in ways that men and boys are not" (134). In this tradition, a large number of participants suggested that papinacolaou or VIA VILI tests, both considered invasive and embarrassing for Kenyan women[9] were easy or routine. The code *ease of screening* was applied 31 times. Those responses were often (12 of 31 occurrences) connected to question 12: "Why are these the most important screenings." Many of them involve excerpts about self or clinical breast exams as an example of screening test that is easily accessible. Others maintain the inexpensiveness of the VIA VILI test, shorthand for visual inspection with acetic acid and/or visual inspection with Lugol's iodine. It replaces a papanicolaou test, using iodine or acetic acid applied directly to the cervix to immediately show lesions rather than requiring laboratory results. One participant suggested "Yeah, it's easier, and most of the people can do it at the dispensary level – at all facilities." While these tests may be performed regularly and cheaply, patients might not find them easy. Additionally, participants sometimes claimed that papanicolaou tests are easy as well, despite the necessity of waiting and paying for lab results, something other participants saw as a challenge. Screenings that require laboratory tests create a barrier for Kenyan health care systems, and yet participants undercut that by suggesting papanicolaou tests specifically are easy four times. A number of participants blur the distinction by listing the category of cervical screening rather than differentiating VIA VILI or papanicolaou in conjunction with the code ease of screening. Yet such screenings are not necessarily *easy* or comfortable for the women who receive them.

Reflecting patterns where men are not asked to undergo invasive tests with the same sanguinity, prostate exams are not routine in Kenya, and prostate tests usually mean expensive PSA blood tests which require labs. Indeed, in one response, a participant said that a DRE (digital rectal exam) to check for prostate enlargement related to cancer, which does not require laboratory results, could only be done if there were symptoms present, saying "it depends on the symptoms. So you *cannot* really do as a screening." Of course, one could use DRE as screening, just as via villa and papanicolaou are used as screenings, but participants in Kenya – much like medical professionals in the US – are squeamish about invasive tests on male bodies, when they have little compunction about them on female bodies. This tendency to assume that tests performed on women are easy may also correspond with Moscucci's observations that "cancer was thought to be primarily a woman's disease because malignancies of breast, cervix, and other 'external' organs were the only ones that could be diagnosed" (2). Suggesting that the cervix is an *external* organ reflects just how pervasive expectations of women's passive permeability become. Such beliefs travel with Western biomedical procedures and in that vein, a participant suggests VIA VILI "is majorly for the lower facilities where without the lab equipped to do some of these tests, and also it's very cheap. It's free. . . . Because like for me PSA, most of the facilities, they don't have the capacity to do that. It's expensive." DRE is not even listed as an option. Other participants did include PSA tests as routine or easy tests "for the PSA and cervical cancer screening, these two are here," suggesting that PSA, but still not the cheaper but invasive DRE, is becoming more routine, just not as quickly as similarly invasive cervical screenings.

Female Reproductive Cancers Require More Attention

A few participants connect ease of screening for women to Kenyan media and popular cancer campaigns. Kenyan campaigns mirror cancer campaigns in the United States, which also focus on female reproductive cancers. These health campaigns construct Kenya's first cancer care infrastructure by tasking women to intervene with screenings. As one participant explained "They [breast and cervical screenings] are the mostly popularized and lots of campaigns have been organized *probably* because the screening procedure is easier and cheaper." This participant both uses ease of screening language and reinforces the idea that more attention has been paid to female reproductive cancers in Kenya than other cancers. The suggestion that popularity and public health attention in the form of health campaigns "probably" follows from ease suggests an understanding that the popularity, attention, and availability of cancer screening tests may not follow from medical need, such as high incidence or mortality rates. It also reflects that screening "popularity" *can* also come from other rhetorical spaces. Sometimes a test's popularity could come from attitudes about gender and subtle decisions about which bodies should be screened. These attitudes can manifest through external subsidy, offered models of health care responsibility, both of which are informed by Western biomedical attention to fertility and population. This participant's pointed use of "probably" provides space for understanding the myriad ways that attitudes about certain cancers infiltrate a culture.

Following globalism's ability to create flows of money, ideas, and attitudes simultaneously, funding for cancers gendered female come before others and sometimes before good incidence and mortality numbers are available, following British and US patterns of addressing female cancers first. Another participant relayed similar information suggesting that screening for cervical cancer and breast are "actually routine and [receive] funding. Like pap smear test, it's really funded" explaining that resources to support those screening tests exist. One participant explained their high ranking of breast and cervical cancer in caus[ing] the most suffering in Kenya with an observation that "the ranking has to do with the cancers that are *most reported especially in mass media*." According to this participant, media in Kenya mainly carry stories of female reproductive cancers, which mirror Moscucci's findings that early "educational campaigns in Britain continued to direct most attention at women, thus creating the impression that men were not at risk from cancer" (102). These suggestions about media and popularized screening hint that early and perhaps outsized attention to female reproductive cancers in Kenya might affect accurate collection of incidence and mortality data. If introduction of screening campaigns for female cancers happen first, then incidence rates will likely increase as women are screened and diagnosed. This tendency fits with other observations that public health decisions about cancer screening and health education campaigns reflect cultural rather than solely medical concerns.

In the previous chapter, the KEMRI report laments that papanicolaou and other cervical cancer screenings are not available in Kenya. A 2012 article "Knowledge and Acceptability of Pap Smears, Self-Sampling and HPV Vaccination among Adult Women in Kenya" affirms that in a sample of 409 in Nairobi "very few women (19% HIV-negative and 11% HIV-positive) reported having had a Pap smear prior to the study" (Rositch et al. 3). In 2016 and 2017 when Kenyan participants were interviewed, this was no longer entirely true. A number of participants in this study mentioned that screening for cervical cancer is common, especially in the capital (Nairobi); they described use of papanicolaou and the VIA VILI screening test. Additionally, Darwinkel et al.'s 2018 study "Evaluating the Role of Clinical Officers in Providing Reproductive Health Services in Kenya" suggests that clinical officers regularly provide both papanicolaou tests and VIA VILI (4). This follows a pattern established in England where "cervical cancer occupies a crucial place in the history of cancer control policies because it was the first malignancy for which mass screening programmes were instituted in the mid-twentieth century" (Moscucci 204). Kenya follows this Western biomedical pattern, and in the intervening years between the Parliament report and the interviews, a number of efforts have increased the screening rate for breast and cervical cancer, including the "National Cervical

Cancer Prevention Program – Strategic Plan 2012–2015" developed by the Ministry of Public Health with help from World Health Organization and USAID (National). Much of the attention to cervical cancer appears to grow out of family planning efforts and the vast energies that went into AIDS prevention and treatment in Eastern Africa in the early 2000s, and much of the impetus for those family planning and AIDS efforts came from WHO, USAID, CDC, and other Western medical organizations in their global outreach.[10] The same efforts towards screening programs for colon cancer or eradication of esophageal cancer are not forthcoming, and it did not appear to be true for other common cancers in Kenya, like prostate cancer, according to participants. As Moscucci conveys, "gender-specific cancers may be easier to 'sell,' but people's low awareness of other common, non-gender-specific cancers, such as bowel cancer, suggests that there are evident hazards in targeting health measures" (285). Thus, the biomedical global flows *selling* gendered cancers impact the ability and desire for Kenyan HCP to screen for and treat cancer in various sites, and those flows carry imbedded assumptions about female reproductive cancers as the most important cancers to address.

The attention to female reproductive cancers appears in a quantitative question, where participants ranked cancer sites; they reverted somewhat to expectations about gender by ranking female cancers highest. Participants answered the question "Which cancers cause the most suffering in Kenya? Please rank order them." The options provided included liver, esophageal, breast, lung, cervical, and other, in that order. In order to avoid pushing respondents to factor gender into their answers, the cancer sites were aggregated as one large list rather than two lists separated by gender. Often times, participants still responded to the question with two lists: one ranking sites of cancer for women, which were often reproductive cancers, and another ranking the sites of cancer for men, not necessarily reproductive cancers.

While interviewees sometimes did not rank each cancer site in the list provided, all 31 participants ranked breast cancer in their response. Breast cancer was the only site that all participants ranked, although 30 also included cervical cancer in the ranking. Breast cancer also garnered the highest mean of 1.58%, because many participants ranked it very high; 16 respondents placing it first. Cervical cancer received the second highest mean of 1.86%. Despite not providing prostate cancer in the list given to participants, it received the third highest mean of 3.35. After reproductive cancers, the next cancer site ranked high in the list was esophageal cancer with a mean of 3.52%. Despite prostate cancer garnering a higher mean ranking, 25 participants included esophageal compared to the 14 who included prostate cancer. In Kenya esophageal cancer is somewhat common – only prostate cancer is more prevalent in Kenyan men – partially because of the local habit of chewing khat or qat leaves[11] (Patel et al.). Outside of khat, which is native to Eastern Africa, medical researchers often connect esophageal cancer to cigarettes, high alcohol intake, obesity, and the human papilloma virus (HPV) (Syrjänen). Participants fittingly identified it as a large part of cancer incidence in Kenya. Beyond those four sites, 22 respondents included both lung and liver cancer in their answers with mean rankings of 4.36% and 4.77% respectively. The other sites that participants ranked, including colon, stomach, ovarian, pancreatic, leukemia, and others had eight or fewer participants including them. While reproductive cancers were high on their lists, respondents still addressed local and cultural realities about cancer incidence in their siting responses. These numbers suggest that reproductive cancers are the first cancer sites in participants' imaginations and that when they think about cancer, they are often thinking about reproductive cancers. By attending specifically to reproductive cancers, participant answers reflect how attitudes about cancer and cancer care remain gendered.

Cancer Care Challenges Remain in Kenya

In addition to information about gender and cancer found in the responses, the health care professionals included a plethora of surprising responses in their answers to open-ended questions, especially the final question: "What else would you like to tell me about cancer?" A number of participants pointed with frustration to the increasing numbers of cancer incidence in Kenya, some asking me if I could explain the numbers. This matches recent attention paid to cancer in Kenyan public health documents including a Parliament report, which states "There are more Cancer cases being reported in Kenya now than 10 years ago, but Studies to determine the reasons for the increased prevalence and incidence are not being conducted" (Departmental Committee on Health 3). Our participants reflected similar concerns about more cancer diagnoses and lack of studies to determine causes. Once a HCP even requested that I conduct research to find out why cancer rates were increasing. Increases in cancer incidence are part of the health care landscape in many African countries. While describing cancer incidence in Botswana, Livingston explains how "epidemiological and institutional attention garnered by the presence of these new cancer patients is beginning to unearth a much broader problem of cancer facilitated by shifting ecological (in the broadest sense) and demographic conditions on the continent" (Livingston 31). As Livingston suggests, increased incidence and mortality rates flow both from changes in ecology and demography, including Eastern Africans achieving longer lifespans, and from the very fact of collecting the data, but there are no definitive answers about cancer increases in Kenya.

Some of the most interesting and frustrating reactions came from the many participants, who expressed consternation at the lack of National and regional government funding for cancer care in Kenya. Some of them suggested that patients eschew treatment like radiation and chemotherapy because of the cost and lack of coverage by the National Hospital Insurance Fund (NHIF). In Kenya many citizens are eligible for government insurance through the NHIF, which covers treatment at public hospitals. Well-off Kenyans supplement NHIF coverage with private health insurance and pay for private hospitals or overseas treatment for cancer. Seven of 31 participants cited financial or economic patient challenges in answer to question 20, "What else do you want to tell me about cancer." They noted these challenges with statements like

> What I can say is that cancer treatment is very expensive, especially, I can only talk in Kenya because I haven't been to other places. . . . The drugs, like chemotherapy drugs are very expensive. Some of the patients can't even afford and they will tell you let me just go home because I can't afford. . . . So, it's expensive and that's the major challenge here in Kenya.

Another participant explains, "because sometimes people will die thinking of how expensive and how costly it would be." As one participant explains, "you know the health care, you have to pay. And, it's for those with money. Many of them, it [foregoing treatment] is because they cannot afford." These participants' expressed ideas about Kenyans' inability to afford might reflect another type of lack of agency.[12] If you cannot pay to treat your cancer, then you do not have a real choice in your response to diagnosis.

Even more than financial challenges for patients – seven instances – they responded to question 20 with answers that include provider challenges 10 times. Those responses connected because provider challenge language usually includes lack of resources as well, as in this answer "Well, in Africa, our main challenge is that we have no resources. . . . When as healthcare providers, we have very little resources to help us do so many investigative procedures and that limits our knowledge and also that limits our practice as clinicians." For Kenyan HCP cancer care represents a significant challenge.

Participants also addressed policy or government in five responses to question 20, suggesting rightly that the health care system is often partially driven by government bodies. They lament a lack of overarching policy, in one case stating "Yeah, the National Cancer Control whatever, the National Cancer Institute, but they're not functional." The idea that government attention to a disease creates change in medical policy, funding, and outcomes is generally true in the US or Kenya, and the lack made these respondents feel helpless. Thus far, much of the funding in Kenya has come from WHO, USAID, and the CDC, in essence creating some lack of agency as a country to determine health priorities. In this way, agency and autonomy become salient at the national level as it does for individuals at the bodily level. International flows provide Kenyans with capital, campaigns, education, and other definitional forms that obscure how local HCPs might alternatively address local health needs.

Notes

1. Participants included doctors, nurses, lab technicians, and others.
2. Other researchers have suggested language as a challenge for patients and medical providers, explaining "the significance of language in understanding cancer diagnosis and particularly so in sub-Saharan contexts like Kenya" (Githaiga 837). The participants in our study did not focus on language as particularly challenging for patients, although participants suggested cultural differences were a challenge for Kenyans accessing cancer care.
3. Some of this data was reported in Mara and Mara "Blending."
4. See Jean Kilbourne "Beauty . . . and the Beast of Advertising" and Jhally and Kilbourne "Killing Us Softly." See also Gervais et al. According to Gervais "when people sexually objectify women, they separate women's sexual body parts or functions from the entire person, reduce the sexual body parts to the status of mere instruments, or regard the sexual body parts as capable of representing the entire person" (743). See also, https://savethetatas.org
5. Two quantitative questions ask specifically about cancer sites, which partially explains the large number of instances. Responses about screening also evoke mentions of cancer sites because screenings differ by site.
6. See also Haile.
7. See Mara "Spreading" for problems with simply naming HPV a "sexually transmitted disease."
8. These references to environmental toxins as cancer-causing agents also match the Departmental Committee on Health's willingness to attribute cancer incidence to environmental toxins more openly than some Western biomedical tendencies to remain focused on individual and genetic risk.
9. See Kivuti-Bitok who maintain "health care workers reported that many clients find the screening procedure too invasive and is viewed as embarrassing and against the African culture" (Kivuti-Bitok et al.).
10. See Vodicka on integrating cervical cancer screening to an HIV clinic (research funded by International Federation of Gynaecology and Obstetrics).
11. Users chew leaves of the catha edulus plant, which act as a stimulant.
12. Offering some good news, one participant suggested that a local cancer center and the government had teamed to offer cancer treatment through NHIF. Further research shows Texas Cancer Center in Nairobi, a private hospital, which was not one of the research sites, indeed accepts NHIF for chemotherapy and radiotherapy. This kind of conflicting information from participants shows how difficult it can be to understand and treat cancer in Kenya. Even medical professionals do not have current information about funding options for treatment.

Works Cited

Comeau, Tammy Duerden. "Gender Ideology and Disease Theory: Classifying Cancer in Nineteenth Century Britain." *Journal of Historical Sociology*, vol. 20, nos. 1–2, 2007, pp. 158–81.

Darwinkel, Marianne Corine et al. "Evaluating the Role of Clinical Officers in Providing Reproductive Health Services in Kenya." *Human Resources for Health*, vol. 16, no. 1, 2018, pp. 1–8.

Departmental Committee on Health, Department of Research, Republic of Kenya National Assembly. "Policy Brief on the Situational Analysis of Cancer in Kenya." Feb. 2011.

Fosket, Jennifer Ruth. "Breast Cancer Risk as Disease: Biomedicalizing Risk." *Biomedicalization: Technoscience, Health, and Illness in the U.S.*, edited by Adele Clarke et al., Duke UP, 2010, pp. 331–52.

Gervais, Sarah J. et al. "Seeing Women as Objects: The Sexual Body Part Recognition Bias." *European Journal of Social Psychology*, vol. 42, no. 6, 2012, pp. 743–53, Web.

Githaiga, Jennifer Nyawira and Leslie Swartz. "You Have a Swelling: The Language of Cancer Diagnosis and Implications for Cancer Management in Kenya." *Patient Education and Counseling*, vol. 100, 2017, pp. 826–38.

Haile, Zelalem, T. et al. "Association Between Risky Sexual Behavior and Cervical Cancer Screening Among Women in Kenya: A Population-Based Study." *Journal of Community Health*, vol. 43, no. 2, 2018, pp. 238–47.

Jhally, Sut et al. *Killing Us Softly 4 Advertising's Image of Women*. Media Education Foundation, 2010.

Kilbourne, Jean. "Beauty . . . and the Beast of Advertising." *Media & Values*, vol. 49, 1990, www.medialit.org/media-values/media-values-articles-42-51.

Kivuti-Bitok, L. et al. "An Exploration of Opportunities and Challenges Facing Cervical Cancer Managers in Kenya." *BMC Research Notes*, vol. 6, 2013, https://doi.org/10.1186/1756-0500-6-136.

Livingston, Julie. *Improvising Medicine: An African Oncology Ward in an Emerging Cancer Epidemic*. Duke UP, 2012.

Mamo, Laura et al. "Producing and Protecting Risky Girlhoods." *Three Shots at Prevention: The HPV Vaccine and the Politics' of Medicine's Simple Solutions*, edited by Keith Wailoo et al., The Johns Hopkins UP, 2010, pp. 121–45.

Mara, Miriam. "Spreading the (Dis)Ease: Gardasil and the Gendering of HPV." *Feminist Formations*, vol. 22, no. 2, 2010, pp. 124–43.

Mara, Miriam and Andrew Mara. "Blending Humanistic and Rhetorical Analysis to Locate Gendered Dimensions of Kenyan Medical Practitioner Attitudes about Cancer." *Technical Communication Quarterly* (*TCQ*), edited by Richard Johnson Sheehan and Elizabeth Angeli, vol. 27, no. 1, 2018, pp. 93–107.

Moscucci, Ornella. *Gender and Cancer in England, 1860–1948*, Palgrave, 2016.

"National Cervical Cancer Prevention Program: Strategic Plan 2012–2015." Ministry of Public Health and Sanitation, and Ministry of Medical Services, www.k4health.org/sites/default/files/National%20Cervical%20Cancer%20Prevention%20Program_Strategic%20Plan.pdf

Ogola, Margaret. *Place of Destiny*. Paulines Publication Africa, 2005.
Patel, J.K. et al. "Drugs of Abuse." Elsevier Science & Technology, 2010, pp. 55–74.
Rositch, Anne F. et al. "Knowledge and Acceptability of Pap Smears, Self-Sampling and HPV Vaccination Among Adult Women in Kenya (Pap Smears, Self-Sampling, and HPV Vaccination)." *PLoS One,* vol. 7, no. 7, 2012, doi:10.1371/journal.pone.0040766.
Sama, Martyn et al. *Governing Health Systems in Africa*. Dakar: Council for the Development of Social Science Research in Africa, 2008. Codesria Book Ser. Web.
Sassen, Saskia. *Territory Authority Rights: From Medieval to Global Assemblages*. Princeton UP, 2006.
Strother, R.M. et al. "The Evolution of Comprehensive Cancer Care in Western Kenya." *Journal of Cancer Policy,* vol. 1, nos. 1–2, 2013, pp. e25–e30, https://doi.org/10.1016/j.jcpo.2013.04.001.
Syrjänen, K.J. "HPV Infections and Oesophageal Cancer." *Journal of Clinical Pathology,* vol. 55, no. 10, 2002, pp. 721–28.
Vodicka, Elisabeth L. et al. "Costs of Integrating Cervical Cancer Screening at an HIV Clinic in Kenya." *International Journal of Gynaecology and Obstetrics: The Official Organ of the International Federation of Gynaecology and Obstetrics,* vol. 136, no. 2, 2017, pp. 220–28.

6 Conclusion
Saratani[1] Going Forward

This book unpacks a biomedical assumption about oncogenic women traced through global flows from Western contexts to Kenyan ones. Women's bodies are constructed as sites of cancer potentiality, through biomedical and cultural practices including medical screening recommendations, medical journal articles, public policy pronouncements, media reports, breast cancer novels, and even postage stamps. We see women's bodies constructed as cancer-producing through the culturescape of Kenyan medicine, by comparing fiction from a medical doctor, medical and policy documents, and interviews with Kenyan Health care providers (HCPs). Tracing the culturescape makes three major contributions to the study of rhetorics of medicine. First, a culturescape investigation, which includes medical, policy, and cultural discourses, provides fuller answers to questions about biomedical interventions and attitudes. Second the analysis that emerges outlines the oncogenic women trope and the ways it manifests through those discourses. Finally, the study traces how global flows transmit biomedicine and its capabilities. In the interviews with HCPs, approaches and ideas that may complicate views about women's oncogenic nature surface, hinting toward useful ways forward. Yet, overall Kenyan introduction of cancer registries and cancer policy follows gendered models developed in the UK and US.

While my work certainly questions screening priorities and marketing, I do not wish to suggest that cancer screenings are not useful in detecting disease. Certainly, screenings have proven to be invaluable. Yet, the inexorable, invasive screening of female bodies has not created an outsize reduction of cancer incidence nor insinuated an eventual cure for cancer. What undue attention to screening female bodies has done is increase early detection, which *can* lead to treatment and extension of life, and breast cancer mortality rates in the US have decreased (Simon). Yet, relentless screening also creates iatrogenic outcomes like false positives and unnecessary fear. Additionally, such screenings continue to construct women's corporeal selves as necessarily available to the medical field for intervention, and sometimes leave men without information about useful screening, potentially undercutting the bioethical principles of autonomy and justice. Documenting the shift of such iatrogenic effects from Western biomedicine into nascent health systems in Kenya suggests that despite rhetorical inroads helping health professionals locate and curb negative ideas about female bodies and autonomy, such attitudes can reappear in new contexts and replay situations that have already been addressed elsewhere.[2] Postcolonial states like Kenya in particular may be susceptible to medical disciplining on the basis of gender as a result of complex interactions around political agency and gender. Ashis Nandy explains that "colonialism, too, was congruent with the existing Western sexual stereotypes and . . . produced a cultural consensus in which political and socio-economic dominance symbolized the dominance of men and masculinity over women and femininity" (4). Nandy's analysis of colonialism read as emasculation (10) explains why postcolonial countries can foreground claims to independence and political power for men after ousting their former colonizers, while building unequal systems that undercut women's political contributions and opportunities. If countries construct achieving independence as regaining masculinity, it leaves little room for female power and authority. Thus postcolonial societies can easily reenact colonial – in this case Western – attitudes about women that undercut autonomy.

Understanding the attitudes that accompany biomedical incursions into Kenya might allow for more critical evaluation of the ways Western influence – especially gender bias – can work against comprehensive effective cancer policy. Biomedicine, like other forms of global movement highlights "the dynamics of interaction and overlap that operate both within the global and the national and between them" (Sassen "Spatialities" 261). The World Health Organization (WHO) operates outside of national strictures, but works alongside national structures like the Ministry of Health in Kenya, aiding policy creation at the national level. Yet the WHO brings more to Kenya than opportunity and cancer screening guidelines. For Kenya to avail itself of such global assemblages and capabilities without assimilating Western biases might require greater attention to the national or indigenous context. In Sassen's model, attention to "territory, authority, and rights" (*Territory* 4) provides some theoretical clarity. For Kenya, authority over their own health policy could involve questioning Western biomedical models and the threats to individual authority (autonomy) they can bring, as well as increased attention to the rights of all embodied persons to choose medical interventions like cancer screening based on personal preferences, rather than merely reserving that right for men. The right to refuse screening could be the logical counterpart to ongoing and growing insistence on the right to *obtain* care, regardless of ability to pay or location.

To build authority and rights, alongside biomedical methods, Kenya's emergent model of medicine could continue to integrate traditional medicine as part of a cohesive cancer plan, especially as KEMRI's scientists isolate medicinal plants used by herbalists for their cancer treatment possibilities. Attending to indigenous and local practices, while integrating useful transmission from elsewhere, assembles existing expertise and familiar patterns, and honors extant ways of knowing. As Christina and Constanze Binder understand "traditional knowledge, which is generally a crucial part of indigenous cultural heritage, can be conceptualised within the capability framework . . . such as the cure of diverse diseases by using traditional knowledge of herbs and plants" (305). KEMRI's hybrid approach of using biomedical scientific models to evaluate medicinal herbs and to appraise traditional healers whose methods and tools are appropriate brings together health approaches that are available in Kenya in creative ways that might be expanded beyond Nairobi.

Kenya's health system might extend authority by attending to the analysis in the Policy Brief on Cancer (Departmental 8–9) and thereby fully address pollution and other environmental issues, protecting citizens from global multinational (and internal) polluters. Regulating pollutants such as plastics that have noted effects on cancer rates, scaffolds approaches they have already begun.[3] Because Kenyans recognize the shifts in cancer prevalence at least partially as pollution related outcomes in earlier policy documents, deepening this analysis, research, and decision-making frame could help shape better cancer policy going forward. We know that "the way a problem is framed constrains the range of possible solutions" (Scott 236), and the Kenyan health system has the opportunity to continue considering cancer risk outside of Condit's "genetic model" and to move beyond what Fosket's critiques as the "individual body as the source of risk" (349). Following those earlier efforts from the Kenyan government to acknowledge the larger ecosystem as part of the cancer challenge and as an alternate space for mediation, they might invest in more stringent pollution controls and fine companies that exceed appropriate guidelines. Those fines could also be used for cancer treatment or research, looping the solutions in with preliminary interventions.

Because Sassen's model underscores rights as a key organizing assemblage, individual rights could help construct stronger cancer policy in Kenya. As evinced in Chapter 2, where the introduction of Gardasil as a gendered intervention proved both detrimental to girl's and women's autonomy and inadequate for reaching herd immunity, biomedical solutions are often predicated on disciplining female bodies. As Kenya integrates new pharmaceutical tools from biomedicine, this tendency traveled with the technology and the 2018 "National Cancer Screening Guidelines"

Conclusion 111

suggests vaccination for girls only. As Kenya works toward eradicating HPV and related disease, they could interrogate assumptions about cancer as a woman's concern and about public health policy predicated on women's (and not men's) responsibility to the public, which removes agency from women and girls. For HPV related cancers, a universal vaccination program for preteen children, not isolating girls for medical interventions, could interrupt its easy transmission. Such an emergent holistic approach could continue to accept useful biomedical transfers from global sources, but refuse to integrate Western biases about women's bodies that skew cancer care practices in directions encouraging female passivity and male agency.

Kenyan HCPs and policy makers might respond to cancer concerns in their country, attending to internal and indigenous epistemologies rather than solely on Western input. For example, the 2018 "Guidelines" builds from Western assumptions about technological intervention as perpetually positive, and advocates for expensive technologically reliant screening like mammography. As Chapter 2 describes, the efficacy of mammograms at certain ages is in question in Western settings, and its iatrogenic outcomes are becoming better understood. Because "users of a policy often hold the greatest insight about its likely and actual effects" (Scott 236), Kenyan policy makers might work with HCPs like the ones I interviewed and invite input from a broad set of Kenyan women to determine breast cancer policy, including and beyond screening. Rather than ceding agency to the mammogram machines, it might be helpful to re-situate autonomy in the patients themselves. Wider conversations could question availability of mammogram machines, costs for hospital facilities and clients, and willingness of women to undergo mammography, as part of a more comprehensive policy making effort. Some breast cancers in Kenya are discovered in very late stages, and earlier detection should be a goal. Yet, asking questions about true prevention or advocating for availability of treatment options, when a diagnosis is made, could be more important goals for some Kenyan women and HCPs.

As this volume contends, biomedical global flows extend "capabilities" including technologies, research, medicines, and training from centers of biomedical innovation like the United States to spaces like Kenya. Yet, Kenya also has local, indigenous capabilities that interact with imported ones, including traditional healing knowledge and practice. How the Kenyan government, medical system, and population integrate, and respond to those Western innovations – with the possibility of rejecting them – becomes a space of inquiry and an opportunity to shape a health system maintaining bioethical principles of autonomy, justice, beneficence, and non-maleficence; and foregrounding authority and rights.

Notes

1. Saratani is the Kiswahili word for cancer. A Kenyan HCP taught it to me my last day in the field collecting interviews.
2. While the US has extended recommendations for Gardasil to boys, Kenya replays their initial mistake of vaccinating only girls, as oncogenic attitudes transfer and re-form.
3. Kenya has already banned plastic bags at grocery stores (Kenya Brings).

Works Cited

Binder, Christina, and Binder, Constanze. "A Capability Perspective on Indigenous Autonomy." *Oxford Development Studies*, vol. 44, no. 3, 2016, pp. 297–314.

Condit, Celeste. "Women's Reproductive Choices and the Genetic Model of Medicine." *Body Talk: Rhetoric, Technology, Reproduction,* edited by Mary M. Lay et al., U of Wisconsin P, 2000, pp. 125–40.

Departmental Committee on Health, Department of Research, Republic of Kenya National Assembly. "Policy Brief on the Situational Analysis of Cancer in Kenya." Feb. 2011.

Fosket, Jennifer Ruth. "Breast Cancer Risk as Disease: Biomedicalizing Risk." *Biomedicalization: Technoscience, Health, and Illness in the U.S.,* edited by Adele Clarke et al., Duke UP, 2010, pp. 331–52.

"Kenya Brings in World's Toughest Plastic Bag Ban: Four Years Jail or $40,000 Fine." *The Guardian,* 28 Aug. 2017.

Ministry of Health, Kenya. "Kenya National Cancer Screening Guidelines." 2018.

Moscucci, Ornella. *Gender and Cancer in England, 1860–1948.* Palgrave, 2016.

Nandy, Ashis. *The Intimate Enemy: Loss and Recovery of Self under Colonialism.* Oxford UP, 1983.

Sassen, Saskia. "Spatialities and Temporalities of the Global: Elements for a Theorization." *Globalization,* edited by Arjun Appadurai, Duke UP, 2001, pp. 260–78.

———. *Territory Authority Rights: From Medieval to Global Assemblages.* Princeton UP, 2006.

Scott, J. Blake. *Risky Rhetoric: Aids and the Cultural Practices of HIV Testing.* Southern Illinois UP, 2003.

Simon, Stacy. "Facts & Figures 2019: US Cancer Death Rate has Dropped 27% in 25 Years." American Cancer Society, www.cancer.org/latest-news/facts-and-figures-2019.html

Appendices

Appendix 1
Instrument

Demographic

Date _____

Medical Role _____

Gender   Male   /   Female

Medical Training   Western Trained   /   Traditional healer or   Both

Age _____

Data

1) Who gets cancer the most?

    A. Men
    B. Women

2) How do you make sense of that?
3) Who suffers the most from cancer in Kenya?

    A. Men
    B. Women

4) How do you respond to that?
5) Who is most likely to die from cancer in Kenya?

    A. Men
    B. Women

6) What do you think about that?

7) Which cancers cause the most suffering in Kenya? Please rank order them – In other words, we will place a 1 next to the one you rank the highest.

   A. Liver _____
   B. Esophogeal _____
   C. Breast _____
   D. Lung _____
   E. Cervical _____
   F. Other _____ _____

8) Is there anything you would like to say about the ranking?
9) Which cancers do you see the most? I would like you to rank order them – In other words, we will place a 1 next to the one you rank the highest.

   A. Liver _____
   B. Esophogeal _____
   C. Breast _____
   D. Lung _____
   E. Cervical _____
   F. Other _____ _____

10) How do you feel about that?
11) What are the three most important cancer screening procedures for Kenyan health?

   1.
   2.
   3.

12) Why are those the most important screenings?
13) What are the three most important prevention measures for Kenyan health?

   1.
   2.
   3.

14) Why are those most important measures?
15) What are the causes of cancer in women?
16) What are the causes of cancer in men?
17) How do you explain cancer to your patients?

18) What is more important for cancer survival?

    A. Medical treatment
    B. Attitude or thought process
    C. Belief system
    D. Other

19) Why do you think that is?
20) What else would you like to tell me about treating people with cancer?

Appendix 2
Code List

Agential/behavioral causes
Participant describes behaviors (by patients) that either lead to cancer or increase cancer risk.

Agential healing
Participant refers to patient behaviors that (they believe) have an effect on treatment or healing outcomes.

Cultural differences
Participant describes something particular about Kenyan culture.

Gender-specific cultural difference
Participant describes something particular to Kenyan culture and gender.

Ease/availability of screening
Participant suggests that a type of screening is easy or readily available.

Emotion
Participant describes personal emotions or uses emotional language.

Identity
Participant refers to something about him- or herself (expertise, personal life) that affects answers.

Expertise
Participant refers to expertise or training.

Personal life
Participant refers to something about personal connection to cancer.

Medical jargon
Participant uses medical or technical language.

Siting
Participant uses language about cancer sites (where on the body cancer occurs).

Passive causes
Participant speaks of risk factors that people (patients) cannot affect or change.

Genetic causes
Participant describes genetic cause of cancer or describes risk in terms of inheritance or genes.

Passive healing
Participant speaks for cancer care that patients do not effect.

Patient challenges
Participant describes challenges for Kenyans in cancer diagnosis and care.

Monetary/financial challenges
Participant describes challenges for patients involving finances or lack of means.

Presenting in late stage challenges
Participant describes how staging and late stage diagnosis presents challenges for patients and treatment.

Presenting in late stage
Participant describes problems that arise from diagnosis at late stage.

Women's status in family
Participant describes diagnosis or treatment challenges arising from women's status in the family.

Provider challenges
Participant describes challenges for providers in diagnosis and treatment of cancer.

Lack of resources
Participant describes how lack of resources affect diagnosis and treatment.

Low levels of screening
Participant describes how low levels of screening effect diagnosis and treatment.

Policy and governmental
Participant describes how government policies and action/lack of action work with/against diagnosis and treatment.

Poor facilities
Participants describes how poor facilities alter diagnosis and treatment.

Provider successes
Participant describes perceived improvements in diagnosis and treatment in the Kenyan context.

Behavioral – what they can do
Participant describes steps providers can or have taken to improve diagnosis and treatment.

Resources
Participant describes how new or improved resources have improved (perceived) diagnosis or treatment outcomes.

Index

Africa: fiction of 50; Western medicine and 52–3; women's illness 50
Africa, cancer in: gender and cancer mortality in Western 9; incidence of 9, 103; mortality by gender 9, 80; WHO and 63, 64, 80, 82–3, 102, 109; *see also* Kenya, cancer in
agency: cancer and female 21, 27, 95–8; cancer and male 21, 95–7; gendered differences in 88; in Kenyan HCP interview study 90, 95–8, 105
agential/behavioral causes (code) 118
agential healing (code) 118
alcohol, gender and health risks from 76–8
American Cancer Society 8, 29
Appadurai, Arjun 11, 12, 21–2
autonomy: as bioethics principle 3, 28, 109, 111; in Kenyan HCP interview study 90, 95–7, 105; medical interventions and 2–4; public health good and men's bodily 35; *see also* women's bodily autonomy

Battlestar Galactica 6
behavioral - what they can do (code) 120
beneficence (bioethics principle) 3, 28, 111
Bernstein, Lennie 30
bioethics ideals or principles 3, 10, 17, 28, 109, 111
biomedical cancer practices, Kenyan cancer culturescape and 46
biomedical culturescapes 108; fiction and 10–12; global movements of biomedical culture 10–13; medical literature and 10–11, 12; US and Kenya 13–14, 15, 111
biomedicalization 2; US trends of 14, 62
Biomedicalization: Technoscience, Health, and Illness in the U.S. (Clarke) 14, 62
biomedicine: globalization of 10–13, 15, 17; oncogenic woman trope in 9, 108; Western 15, 16, 45, 62, 65–8, 81–3, 109, 111
BMJ see British Medical Journal
breast cancer: in cancer culturescape 22–30; in fiction 22, 23, 24–5; Kenyan cancer care and 76, 77, 111; Kenyan National Assembly *Policy Brief* on risk of 76, 77; in men 39n5; overdiagnosis of 27–9, 30, **31**, 38, 39n7; postal stamp 25–6, *26*; US 23
breast cancer exams and screenings 72, 73; *see also* mammograms
breast cancer fears: cancer culturescape and 25–30; mammograms and 27–30; marketing and 23–4
breast cancer research 23–4
British Medical Journal (*BMJ*) 27, 28, 29
burden of disease 34, 40n12

cancer, connection between tumor and 8; *see also specific topics*
cancer, gender and 7, 51; African incidence of 9; African mortality rates of 9, 80; agency and 21; behavior modification and prevention of 76–8; cancer culturescape and

21–2; cancer screenings and 21, 70–85, 99–100; Western Africa, mortality and 9; Western thought on mind body separation and 55–6; *see also* female cancer; Kenyan cancer care, gender and; male cancer
cancer as feminine: policies and 9; women's reproduction and 7–8, 17n6; *see also* female cancer
cancer culturescapes: biomedical and cultural production in 22; breast cancer fears and 25–30; breast cancer in 22–30; cancer, gender and 21–2; global 22; Kenyan 46, 62, 108, 109; US 21, 22; Western 39
cancer incidence: in Africa 9, 103; environmental factors 105n8; in Kenya 62–3, 103
cancer mortality: in Africa by gender 9, 80; Western Africa, gender and 9
cancer prevention: behavior modification, gender and 76–8; screenings and 27, 28, 70–5
cancer registries 14, 63; *see also* Kenyan cancer registries
cancer research: for all sites but skin 9, 17n7; breast 23–4; IARC 14, 63, 68; *see also* Kenyan cancer research
cancer screenings: colonoscopy 71; cost/benefit analyses of 39n6; genetic testing 72; Kenyan reports and documents on 70–85; prevention and 27, 28, 70–5
cancer screenings, gender and 21, 70–85, 99–100; *see also* female cancer screenings; male cancer screenings
cancer sites: in cancer research 9, 17n7; *Place of Destiny* and 55–6; siting code in Kenyan HCP interview study 95, 105n5, 119
capacities, reproductive 7, 38, 51
Center for Traditional Medicine and Drug Research (CTMDR) 66
cervical cancer 7; fear of 34; HPV and 33, 34–5, 37, 82–3; papanicolaou testing for 9, 25, 34, 71, 72, 73, 85n5, 85n9, 99, 101
cesarean section (C-section) 1, 3–4

Clarke, Adele 2, 3, 11, 63, 65; *Biomedicalization: Technoscience, Health, and Illness in the U.S.* 14, 62
clinical trials, for Gardasil 34, 35
code list 118–20
Cole, Catherine 47
colonialism, gender and 109
colonoscopy 71
Coly, Ayo 60n1
Comeau, Tammy Duerden 7, 8, 92
compulsory treatment, cesarean sections and 1, 3–4; *see also* medical interventions
concatenation 21–2
Condit, Celeste 4, 6, 8, 75
C-section *see* cesarean section
CTMDR *see* Center for Traditional Medicine and Drug Research
cultural differences (code) 118
culturescape: biomedical 10–15, 108, 111; concept of 11; oncogenic woman trope and 10–11, 15–16; *see also* cancer culturescapes

Diamant, Anita 22, 24–5
digital rectal exam (DRE) 40n14, 69, 99, 100
disease: burden of 34, 40n12; gestational trophoblastic 17n6
DRE *see* digital rectal exam
Dubriwny, Tasha 11

ease/availability of screening (code) 99–100, 118
efficacy: of mammograms 27–30; testing for 35
Eldoret Cancer Registry 16, 64, 68; data, documents and reports 65, 69–70, 79–81, 84; Kenyan National Assembly documents and 81; NCR and 79, 81
emotion (code) 118
environment, cancer and: cancer incidence and 105n8; Kenyan cancer care and 63, 75, 79, 83, 85n8, 110, 112n3; Kenyan National Assembly *Policy Brief* on 79, 83
Epstein, Julia 5, 12
expertise (code) 118

female agency: cancer and 21, 27, 95–8; in Kenyan HCP interview study 95–8
female cancer: beliefs about weakness of women's bodies and 7, 8, 38; female agency and 21, 27; funding priority for 101; male cancer and 8, 21; in popular culture 5–6; popular imagery juxtaposition of male injury versus 5–6; women's bodily autonomy and 9, 21, 27; see also breast cancer; cancer, gender and; cancer as feminine; cervical cancer
female cancer fears: breast cancer 23–30; cancer culturescape and 25–30; cervical cancer 34; disciplining of women's bodies and 21, 38–9; as sexually transmitted disease 21
female cancer screenings 108; Kenyan HCP interview study on 99–102, 105n5, 105n8; oncogenic woman trope and 9; papanicolaou testing 9, 25, 34, 71, 72, 73, 85n5, 85n9, 99, 101; women's bodily autonomy and 9, 21, 26–7; see also breast cancer exams and screenings
female sexuality: beliefs about weakness of women's bodies and 33; objectification of 105n4
feminist texts: of Ogola 47–51; *Place of Destiny* as anti-feminist and 47–51, 60
fiction: biomedical culturescape and 10–12; breast cancer in 22, 23, 24–5; medical literature and 10–12; see also Kenyan fiction
Finnegan, Cara 13
Fosket, Jennifer Ruth 70, 75
Foucault, Michel 1–2, 3, 21, 78

Gardasil vaccine 16, 30–2, 34–8, 112n2
gender: colonialism and 109; health rhetorics and 4–5; health risks from alcohol and 76–8; medical documents, Western medicine, and identities of 14; *Place of Destiny*, gender and 16, 46, 51–60, 92, 95; see also cancer, gender and

Gender and Cancer in England, 1860–1948 (Moscucci) 7
gender bias: in brain sex research 6; globalization of biomedicine and 15, 17; Kenyan cancer registries and 69–85
gender-specific cultural difference (code) 118
genetic causes (code) 119
Gervais, Sarah J. 105n4
gestational trophoblastic disease 17n6
Gilman, Sander 6
"Global Cancer Statistics" 8
global healthscapes: cancer culturescapes 22; oncogenic woman trope and 9–10
globalization of biomedicine: gendered body biases and 15, 17; global movements of biomedical culture 10–13
global mobility, of oncogenic identities 13–17
Good Harbor (Diamant) 22, 24–5
Grosz, Elizabeth 4
Gusii 66–8

Hausman, Bernice L. 5
Hayles, N. Katherine 12
health care, legal and cultural barriers to 10
health rhetoricians 4–5
health rhetorics: gender and 4–5; research on 4–5; two-sex dualism and 4
healthscapes 11; cancer care in Kenyan 62; global 9–10, 22; oncogenic woman trope and global 9–10
herbalists, Kenyan 65–6, 68
herbal remedies/medicinal plants, Kenyan 66, 68, 85n3
herd immunity 37
Hinkle, Judge 1
Hirschauer, Stefan 4
HIV testing, of pregnant women 1
Holloway, Karla 3, 12, 24, 59, 60n1, 72
How We Become Posthuman (Hayles) 12
Human Papilloma Virus (HPV) 30–5, 37–8, 40nn9–10, 82–3

IARC *see* International Agency for Research on Cancer
iatrogenic effects of care 29
identities: global mobility of oncogenic 13–17; medical documents, Western medicine and gendered 14
identity (code) 118
immunogenicity, for HPV 34
incidence (rates of disease) *see* cancer incidence
International Agency for Research on Cancer (IARC) 14, 63, 68

JAMA see Journal of American Medical Association
Jemal, Ahmedin 8
Journal of American Medical Association (JAMA) 28, 29
justice (bioethics principle) 3, 10, 17, 28, 109, 111

KEMRI *see* Kenya Medical Research Institute
Kenya: biomedical culturescapes of US and 13–14, 15, 111; oncology centers 68, 70; overview 45
Kenya, cancer in: campaigns 63, *64*; HPV 82–3; incidence of 62–3, 103; WHO and 63, 64, 82–3, 102, 109
Kenya, gender and: cancer reports and documents 16, 69–85; inequities 47, 48; medical disciplining of 109; *Place of Destiny* and 47–55
Kenya Medical Research Institute (KEMRI) 16, 63–4, 68, 110; CTMDR 66; Kenyan National Assembly *Policy Brief* and data from 76–8; *see also* Nairobi Cancer Registry
Kenyan cancer care: biomedical infrastructure 14, 45, 64, 65; breast cancer 76, 77, 111; environmental care and 63, 75, 79, 83, 85n8, 110, 112n3; funding 101, 104, 105n12; Kenyan healthscapes and 62; Kenyan traditional healing and 65–8; Kenyan traditional medicines and 62, 66–8, 110; North American cancer care and 14, 39; Western biomedicine and 16, 45, 62, 65–8, 81–3, 109, 111

Kenyan cancer care, gender and 51, 110; Kenyan HCPs and 16–17, 88–103, 111; Western cancer technologies and 16, 88
Kenyan cancer culturescape: biomedical cancer practices and 46; Kenyan fiction and 46; oncogenic woman trope and 62, 108, 109
Kenyan cancer registries 16; data, documents and reports 14, 63, 65, 68–83; gendered bias and 69–84; oncogenic woman trope and 65, 68, 73, 84; overview 68–9; passive acquisition of cancer in females and documents of 65, 76, 77; screenings, prevention, gendered biases and recommendations in reports from 70–85; *see also* Eldoret Cancer Registry; Nairobi Cancer Registry
Kenyan cancer reports and documents: cancer screenings in 70–85; gender and 16, 69–85; Kenyan National Assembly *Policy Brief* 63–4, 75–9, 83, 84; oncogenic woman trope in 65, 68, 73, 78, 79, 82–4; of WHO 82–3; *see also* Kenyan cancer registries
Kenyan cancer research 62; on traditional healing 66–8; on traditional medicines 66, 68, 110; *see also* Kenya Medical Research Institute; Kenyan cancer registries; Kenyan HCP interview study
Kenyan fiction, Kenyan cancer culturescape and 46; *see also* Ogola, Margaret; *Place of Destiny*
Kenyan HCP interview study: agency theme 90, 95–8, 105; autonomy theme 90, 95–7, 105; codes 118–20; on female cancer screenings 99–102, 105n5, 105n8; on female reproductive cancers requiring more attention 100–3; instrument questions 89, 115–17; on men eschewing health care and dying more from cancer 90, 92–5; on men retaining agency 95–7; methods 88–90, 105nn1–2; overview 16–17, 88; on passive acquisition of cancer in females 95–100; on remaining

cancer care challenges 103–5; research site *89*; on women getting and suffering more from cancer 90, *91*, 92–5; on women having limited autonomy 95–7; on women's increased availability for screening 99–100
Kenyan health care providers (Kenyan HCPs): Kenyan cancer care, gender and 16–17, 88–103, 111; *see also* Kenyan HCP interview study
Kenyan health insurance: availability 65; NHIF 65, 103, 105n12
Kenyan healthscapes, cancer care in 62
Kenyan Ministry of Health, "National Cancer Screening Guidelines" 83–4
Kenyan National Assembly: Eldoret Cancer Registry documents and 81; *Policy Brief on the Situational Analysis of Cancer in Kenya* 63–4, 75–9, 83, 84
Kenyan traditional healers 85n4; cancer treatment by 66–8; herbalists 65–6, 68
Kenyan traditional healing: cancer care and 65–8; cancer research on 66–8
Kenyan traditional medicines: cancer care and 62, 66–8, 110; cancer research on 66, 68, 110; CTMDR 66; herbal remedies/medicinal plants 66, 68, 85n3
Keränen, Lisa 13
khat, chewing 74, 85n7, 103, 105n11
Kimball, Anne S. 37, 40n9
Kipsigis 66–8
Kivuti-Bitok, L. 90
Komen Foundation 22, 23, 24
Kristeva, Julia 8

lack of resources (code) 119
Laryngeal papillomas 33, 40n11
Lay, Mary M. 8
Less Noble Sex, The (Tuana) 6
liver cancer 76–7
Livingston, Julie 39, 80, 83, 103
Lost (television series) 5, 17n4
low levels of screening (code) 120
Lund, Giuliana 50

Maathai, Wangari 63
Mackenzie, Catriona 36

male agency: cancer and 21, 95–7; in Kenyan HCP interview study 95–7
male cancer: breast cancer 39n5; female cancer and 8, 21; male agency and 21; narratives of 23; *see also* cancer, gender and
male cancer screenings 9; prostate 9, 21, 23, 29, 39n1, 39n8, 40n14, 69, 72, 73, 99, 100
males: HPV and 32–3, 34, 35, 37, 38, 82–3; popular imagery juxtaposition of female cancer versus injury of 5–6; vaccines for 30, 32–8
mammograms 38; breast cancer fears and 27–30; disciplining of women's bodies through 22; efficacy of 27–30, 111; harm of 28, 29, 30, **31**; tumor detection by 27, 28
Mamo, L. 2, 4, 74, 99
Mayo Clinic 38
medical documents: gendered identities, Western medicine and 14; *see also* Kenyan cancer reports and documents
medical interventions: autonomy and 2–4; justifications 3; for men 4, 10, 37; *Place of Destiny* and gendered control of 56–60; public health and 2–3; women's 1–4, 10, 37
medicalization: biomedicalization 2, 14, 62; definition 2; women's over- 36, 40n15
medical jargon (code) 119
medical literature: biomedical culturescape and 10–11, 12; fiction and 10–12
medical penetrations, women's bodily autonomy and 36, 37
men: genital treatment 35; medical interventions for 4, 10, 37; public health good and bodily autonomy of 35; *see also* gender; males
men's medical treatment 36; physicals 35, 40n14
Miller, Anthony 27
Miller, Sarah Alison 8
Modernity at Large (Appadurai) 21–2
monetary/financial challenges (code) 119
mortality (rates of disease) *see* cancer mortality

Index

Moscucci, Ornella 7, 9, 51, 71, 80, 92, 101, 102
Mutuma, Geoffrey 14, 64, 73

Nairobi Cancer Registry (NCR) 16, 64; data, documents and reports 14, 63, 69–75, 79–81, 83, 84; Eldoret Cancer Registry and 79, 81; Kenyan National Assembly *Policy Brief* and data from 76; reproductive cancers in reports of 73, 80
Nairobi hospitals 45
Nakumatt cancer awareness campaign 63, *64*
Nandy, Ashis 109
National Health Insurance Fund (NHIF) 65, 103, 105n12
NCR *see* Nairobi Cancer Registry
New England Journal of Medicine (NEJM) 28, 29
NHIF *see* National Health Insurance Fund
non-maleficence (bioethics principle) 3, 111
North American cancer care 14, 39

Odhiambo, Tom 47
Ogola, Margaret: feminist texts of 47–51; fiction of 46; Kenyan cancer culturescape and fiction of 46; *The River and the Source* 46, 51; *see also Place of Destiny*
oncogenic identities, global mobility of 13–17
oncogenic woman trope: in biomedicine 9, 108; cancer screenings and 9; changing assumptions about 38; culturescape and 10–11, 15–16; global healthscapes and 9–10; Kenyan cancer culturescape and 62, 108; Kenyan cancer registries and 65, 68, 73, 84; in Kenyan cancer reports and documents 65, 68, 73, 78, 79, 82–4; in Kenyan National Assembly *Policy Brief* 78, 79, 84; in *Place of Destiny* 50, 54–5, 60; public health as women's responsibility and 9; vaccines and 30, 38; women's reproduction and 8

oncology centers, Kenyan 68, 70
oral tumors 76–7
overdiagnosis, of breast cancer 27–9, 30, **31**, 38, 39n7
Owens, Kim H. 5

Papanicolaou, George 25
papanicolaou testing 9, 25, 34, 71, 72, 73, 85n5, 85n9, 99, 101
passive acquisition of cancer, in females 8; Kenyan cancer registry documents and 65, 76, 77; in *Place of Destiny* 16, 57, 92, 95
passive causes (code) 119
passive healing (code) 119
pathologization 4, 71
patient challenges (code) 119
Pemberton, Laura 1
Pemberton *vs.* Tallahassee Memorial Regional Center 1
Perry, Rick 30–1, 32–3, 36, 40n10
personal life (code) 118
Place of Destiny (Ogola): beliefs about weakness of women's bodies in 58–60; as feminist and antifeminist text 47–51, 60; gendered representations of cancer in 16, 46, 51–60, 92, 95; Kenya, gender and 47–55; medical interventions and gendered control of treatment in 56–60; medical personnel in 52–3; oncogenic woman trope in 50, 54–5, 60; overview 46–7; passive acquisition of cancer in females in 16, 57, 92, 95; sites of cancer in 55–6; tumors in 51, 54, 55; Western thought on mind body separation and 55–6
policy and governmental (code) 120
Policy Brief on the Situational Analysis of Cancer in Kenya 63–4, 75–9, 83, 84
poor facilities (code) 120
postal stamps, cancer 25–6, *26*
presenting in late stage (code) 119
presenting in late stage challenges (code) 119
prevention 26; cancer 27, 28, 70–8
Private Bodies, Public Lives (Holloway) 12

"Producing and Protecting Risky Girlhoods" (Mamo) 2
prostate cancer screenings 9, 21, 23, 29, 39n1, 39n8, 40n14, 69, 72, 73, 99, 100
Prostate-Specific Antigen (PSA) tests 9, 39n1, 39n8, 40n14, 69, 72, 100
provider challenges (code) 119
provider successes (code) 120
PSA tests *see* Prostate-Specific Antigen tests
public health: medical interventions in 2–3; men's bodily autonomy and 35
public health, as women's responsibility 4; medical interventions and 2, 10, 37; oncogenic woman trope and 9

Reagan, Leslie 7, 35, 36
Reinventing the Sexes: The Biomedical Construction of Femininity and Masculinity (Wijngaard) 9, 51
reproduction, Western obsession with African 80; *see also* women's reproduction
reproductive cancers, female 21; in Kenyan HCP interview study 100–3; *see also* breast cancer; cervical cancer
reproductive cancers, in NCR reports 73, 80
resources (code) 120
River and the Source, The (Ogola) 46, 51
Rubella vaccine 3, 17n3

saratani (cancer) 108, 112n1
Sassen, Saskia 12, 14, 15, 109, 112n3
Scott, J. Blake 1, 4, 5, 13
screening: ease/availability of 99–100, 118; low levels of 120; *see also* cancer screenings
Segal, Judy 4
Selleck, Laurie 23, 29
sex: female cancer fears as sexually transmitted disease 21; female sexuality 33, 105n4; health rhetorics and two-sex dualism 4; *The Less Noble Sex* 6; *Reinventing the Sexes* 9, 51
Shaw, Susan 36
sites of cancer *see* cancer sites
siting (code) 95, 105n5, 119
Stacey, Jackie 8

Tallahassee Memorial Regional Center 1
Tanaka, Kiyofumi 66–7
Tenge, C. N. 79, 81
Teratologies (Kristeva) 8
Teston, Christa 7
Thompson, Marie 31, 35
traditional medicine 15, 65; *see also* Kenyan traditional medicines
Tuana, Nancy 6
tumors: connection between cancer and 8; oral 76–7; in *Place of Destiny* 51, 54, 55

United Nations (UN), "Right of Everyone to the Enjoyment of the Highest Attainable Standard of Physical and Mental Health" report 10
United States (US): biomedical culturescapes of Kenya and 13–14, 15, 111; biomedicalization trends 14, 62; breast cancer in 23; gender and cancer culturescape of 21, 22
United States Preventive Services Task Force (USPSTF) 29

vaccines: Gardasil 16, 30–2, 34–8, 112n2; HPV 30–5, 37, 38, 40nn9–10; for males 30, 32–8; Rubella 3, 17n3; Texas and 16, 30–5
vaccines for females: female-only mandates for 3, 17n3, 30–5, 36, 40nn9–10; Gardasil 16, 30–2, 34–8, 112n2; HPV 30–5, 37, 38, 40nn9–10; oncogenic woman trope and 30, 38; vaccines for males and 30, 32–8
Verbrugge, Lois 36

Wailoo, Keith 33
Washington Post 29, 30
Western biomedicine 15; Kenyan cancer care and 16, 45, 62, 65–8, 81–3, 109, 111
Western cancer culturescape 39
Western cancer technologies 16, 88
Western medicine: Africa and 52–3; gendered identities, medical documents and 14

Western thought, on mind body separation: cancer, gender and 55–6; *Place of Destiny* and 55–6
Western world, African reproduction and 80
Wheeler, Cosette 35, 40n14
Whitehead, Anne 12
WHO *see* World Health Organization
Wijngaard, Marianne Van Den 9, 12, 51
women, science and 5; *see also* gender; *specific topics*
women's bodies: disciplining of 21, 22, 38–9; pathologization of 4, 71; sexual objectification of 105n4
women's bodies, beliefs about weakness of 24; female cancer and 7, 8, 38; female sexuality and 33; infantilization of adult women patients in 59–60; in Kenyan National Assembly *Policy Brief* 76; laboratory and 6; in *Place of Destiny* 58–60
women's bodily autonomy: cancer and 9, 21, 27; cancer screenings and 9, 21, 26–7; limits on 1–4, 5, 35; medical interventions and 2–4, 10, 37; medical penetrations and 36, 37; medical treatment and 35–6
women's medical interventions: pregnant women and 1, 3–4; public health as women's responsibility and 2, 10, 37; women's bodily autonomy and 2–4, 10, 37
women's medical treatment: bodily autonomy and 35–6; over-medicalization 36, 40n15; of reproductive and sexual organs 35
women's reproduction: cancer as feminine and 7–8, 17n6; medical interventions and pregnant women 1, 3–4; medical treatment of reproductive and sexual organs 35; oncogenic woman trope and 8
women's status in family (code) 119
World Health Organization (WHO) 14; cancer in Africa and 63, 64, 80, 82–3, 102, 109; cancer in Kenya and 63, 64, 82–3, 102, 109